Canto is an imprint offering a range of titles, classic and more recent, across a broad spectrum of subject areas and interests. History, literature, biography, archaeology, politics, religion, psychology, philosophy and science are all represented in Canto's specially selected list of titles, which now offers some of the best and most accessible of Cambridge publishing to a wider readership.

AN
EXPERIMENT IN
CRITICISM

AN
EXPERIMENT IN
CRITICISM

BY

C. S. LEWIS

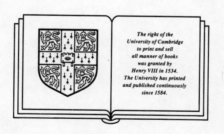

The right of the
University of Cambridge
to print and sell
all manner of books
was granted by
Henry VIII in 1534.
The University has printed
and published continuously
since 1584.

CAMBRIDGE UNIVERSITY PRESS

CAMBRIDGE
NEW YORK   PORT CHESTER
MELBOURNE   SYDNEY

Published by the Press Syndicate of the University of Cambridge
The Pitt Building, Trumpington Street, Cambridge CB2 1RP
40 West 20th Street, New York, NY 10011–4211, USA
10 Stamford Road, Oakleigh, Victoria 3166, Australia

First published 1961
Reprinted 1965 1969 1973 1976 1978 1979 1983 1985 1987 1988
Canto edition 1992

Printed in Great Britain at the University Press, Cambridge

A catalogue record for this book is available from the British Library

Library of Congress cataloguing in publication data applied for

ISBN 0 521 42281 7 paperback

CONTENTS

I

THE FEW AND THE MANY

IN this essay I propose to try an experiment. Literary criticism is traditionally employed in judging books. Any judgement it implies about men's reading of books is a corollary from its judgement on the books themselves. Bad taste is, as it were by definition, a taste for bad books. I want to find out what sort of picture we shall get by reversing the process. Let us make our distinction between readers or types of reading the basis, and our distinction between books the corollary. Let us try to discover how far it might be plausible to define a good book as a book which is read in one way, and a bad book as a book which is read in another.

I think this worth trying because the normal procedure seems to me to involve almost continually a false implication. If we say that *A* likes (or has a taste for) the women's magazines and *B* likes (or has a taste for) Dante, this sounds as if *likes* and *taste* have the same meaning when applied to both; as if there were a single activity, though the objects to which it is directed are different. But observation convinces me that this, at least usually, is untrue.

Already in our schooldays some of us were making our first responses to good literature. Others, and these the majority, were reading, at school, *The Captain*, and, at home, short-lived novels from the circulating library. But it was apparent then that the majority did not 'like' their fare in the way we 'liked' ours. It is apparent still. The differences leap to the eye.

In the first place, the majority never read anything twice. The sure mark of an unliterary man is that he considers 'I've read it already' to be a conclusive argument against reading a work. We have all known women who remembered a novel so dimly that they had to stand for half an hour in the library skimming through it before they were certain they had once read it. But the moment they became certain, they rejected it immediately. It was for them dead, like a burnt-out match, an old railway ticket, or yesterday's paper; they had already used it. Those who read great works, on the other hand, will read the same work ten, twenty or thirty times during the course of their life.

Secondly, the majority, though they are sometimes frequent readers, do not set much store by reading. They turn to it as a last resource. They abandon it with alacrity as soon as any alternative pastime turns up. It is kept for railway journeys, illnesses, odd moments of enforced solitude, or for the process called 'reading oneself to sleep'. They sometimes combine it with desultory conversation; often, with listening to the radio. But literary people are always looking for leisure and silence in which to

2

read and do so with their whole attention. When they are denied such attentive and undisturbed reading even for a few days they feel impoverished.

Thirdly, the first reading of some literary work is often, to the literary, an experience so momentous that only experiences of love, religion, or bereavement can furnish a standard of comparison. Their whole consciousness is changed. They have become what they were not before. But there is no sign of anything like this among the other sort of readers. When they have finished the story or the novel, nothing much, or nothing at all, seems to have happened to them.

Finally, and as a natural result of their different behaviour in reading, what they have read is constantly and prominently present to the mind of the few, but not to that of the many. The former mouth over their favourite lines and stanzas in solitude. Scenes and characters from books provide them with a sort of iconography by which they interpret or sum up their own experience. They talk to one another about books, often and at length. The latter seldom think or talk of their reading.

It is pretty clear that the majority, if they spoke without passion and were fully articulate, would not accuse us of liking the wrong books, but of making such a fuss about any books at all. We treat as a main ingredient in our well-being something which to them is marginal. Hence to say simply that they like one thing and we another is to leave out nearly the whole of the facts. If *like* is the correct word for what they do to books, some other word must be found for what we do. Or, conversely, if we *like* our kind of book we must not say that they *like* any book. If the few have 'good taste', then we may have to say that no such thing as 'bad taste' exists: for the inclination which the many have to their sort of reading is not the same thing and, if the word were univocally used, would not be called taste at all.

Though I shall concern myself almost entirely with literature, it is worth noting that the same difference of attitude is displayed about the other arts and about natural beauty. Many people enjoy popular music in a way which is compatible with humming the tune, stamping in time, talking, and eating. And when the popular tune has once gone out of fashion they enjoy it no more. Those who enjoy Bach react quite differently. Some buy pictures because the walls 'look so bare without them'; and after the pictures have been in the house for a week they become practically invisible to them. But there are a few who feed on a great picture for years. As regards nature, the majority 'like a nice view as well as anyone'. They are not saying a word against it. But to make the landscapes a really important factor in, say, choosing the place for a holiday—to put them on a level with such serious considerations as a luxurious hotel, a good golf links, and a sunny climate—would seem to them affectation. To 'go on' about them like Wordsworth would be humbug.

II

FALSE CHARACTERISATIONS

IT is, in the logical sense, an 'accident' that readers of the one kind are many and those of the other few, and the two kinds are not characterised by these numerical terms. Our business is with different ways of reading. Common observation has already enabled us to make a rough and ready description, but we must try to penetrate further. The first step is to eliminate some hasty identifications of the 'few' and the 'many'.

Some critics write of those who constitute the literary 'many' as if they belonged to the many in every respect, and indeed to the rabble. They accuse them of illiteracy, barbarism, 'crass', 'crude' and 'stock' responses which (it is suggested) must make them clumsy and insensitive in all the relations of life and render them a permanent danger to civilisation. It sometimes sounds as if the reading of 'popular' fiction involved moral turpitude. I do not find this borne out by experience. I have a notion that these 'many' include certain people who are equal or superior to some of the few in psychological health, in moral virtue, practical prudence, good manners, and general adaptability. And we all know very well that we, the literary, include no small

5

percentage of the ignorant, the caddish, the stunted, the warped, and the truculent. With the hasty and wholesale *apartheid* of those who ignore this we must have nothing to do.

If it had no other defect it would still be too dia-grammatic. The two sorts of readers are not cut off by immovable barriers. Individuals who once be-longed to the many are converted and join the few. Others desert from the few to the many, as we often sadly discover on meeting an old schoolfellow. Those who are on the 'popular' level as regards one art may be deeply appreciative of another; musicians sometimes have deplorable preferences in poetry. And many whose responses to all the arts are trivial may yet be people of great intelligence, learning and subtlety.

This latter phenomenon does not surprise us much because their learning is of a different sort from ours, and the subtlety of a philosopher or physicist is different from that of a literary person. What is more surprising and disquieting is the fact that those who might be expected *ex officio* to have a profound and permanent appreciation of literature may in reality have nothing of the sort. They are mere professionals. Perhaps they once had the full response, but the 'hammer, hammer, hammer on the hard, high road' has long since dinned it out of them. I am thinking of unfortunate scholars in foreign universities who cannot 'hold down their jobs' unless they repeatedly publish articles each of

6

which must say, or seem to say, something new about some literary work; or of overworked reviewers, getting through novel after novel as quickly as they can, like a schoolboy doing his 'prep'. For such people reading often becomes mere work. The text before them comes to exist not in its own right but simply as raw material; clay out of which they can complete their tale of bricks. Accordingly we often find that in their leisure hours they read, if at all, as the many read. I well remember the snub I once got from a man to whom, as we came away from an examiners' meeting, I tactlessly mentioned a great poet on whom several candidates had written answers. His attitude (I've forgotten the words) might be expressed in the form 'Good God, man, do you want to go on *after hours*? Didn't you hear the hooter blow?' For those who are reduced to this condition by economic necessity and overwork I have nothing but sympathy. Unfortunately, ambition and combativeness can also produce it. And, however it is produced, it destroys appreciation. The 'few' whom we are seeking cannot be identified with the *cognoscenti*. Neither Gigadibs nor Dryasdust is necessarily among them.

Still less is the status seeker. As there are, or were, families and circles in which it was almost a social necessity to display an interest in hunting, or county cricket, or the Army List, so there are others where it requires great independence not to talk about, and therefore occasionally to read, the

7

approved literature, especially the new and astonishing works, and those which have been banned or have become in some other way subjects of controversy. Readers of this sort, this 'small vulgar', act in one respect exactly like those of the 'great vulgar'. They are entirely dominated by fashion. They drop the Georgians and begin to admire Mr Eliot, acknowledge the 'dislodgement' of Milton, and discover Hopkins, at exactly the right moment. They will not like your book if the dedication begins with *To* instead of *For*. Yet, while this goes on downstairs, the only real literary experience in such a family may be occurring in a back bedroom where a small boy is reading *Treasure Island* under the bed-clothes by the light of an electric torch.

The devotee of culture is, as a person, worth much more than the status seeker. He reads as he also visits art galleries and concert rooms, not to make himself acceptable, but to improve himself, to develop his potentialities, to become a more complete man. He is sincere and may be modest. Far from trotting along obediently with the fashion, he is more likely to stick too exclusively to the 'established authors' of all periods and nations, 'the best that has been thought and said in the world'. He makes few experiments and has few favourites. Yet this worthy man may be, in the sense I am concerned with, no true lover of literature at all. He may be as far from that as a man who does exercises

8

with dumb-bells every morning may be from being a lover of games. The playing of games will ordinarily contribute to a man's bodily perfection; but if that becomes the sole or chief reason for playing them they cease to be games and become 'exercise'.

No doubt, a man who has a taste for games (and for overeating as well) may very properly act on the medical motive when he makes for himself a rule to give general priority to his taste for games. In the same way, a man who has a gust both for good literature and for mere time-killing with trash may reasonably, on cultural grounds, on principle, give a priority to the former. But in both instances we are presupposing a genuine gust. The first man chooses football rather than a gargantuan lunch because the game, as well as the lunch, is one of the things he enjoys. The second turns to Racine instead of E. R. Burroughs because *Andromaque*, as well as *Tarzan*, is really attractive to him. But to come to the particular game with nothing but a hygienic motive or to the tragedy with nothing but a desire for self-improvement, is not really to play the one or to receive the other. Both attitudes fix the ultimate intention on oneself. Both treat as a means something which must, while you play or read it, be accepted for its own sake. You ought to be thinking about goals not about 'fitness'. Your mind ought to be absorbed—and, if so, what time have you for so bleak an abstraction as Culture?— in that spiritual chess where 'passions exquisitely carved in alexandrines' are the pieces and human beings are the squares.[1]

This laborious sort of misreading is perhaps especially prevalent in our own age. One sad result of making English Literature a 'subject' at schools and universities is that the reading of great authors is, from early years, stamped upon the minds of conscientious and submissive young people as something meritorious. When the young person in question is an agnostic whose ancestors were Puritans, you get a very regrettable state of mind. The Puritan conscience works on without the Puritan theology—like millstones grinding nothing; like digestive juices working on an empty stomach and producing ulcers. The unhappy youth applies to literature all the scruples, the rigorism, the self-examination, the distrust of pleasure, which his forebears applied to the spiritual life; and perhaps soon all the intolerance and self-righteousness. The doctrine of Dr I. A. Richards in which the correct reading of good poetry has a veritable therapeutic value confirms him in this attitude. The Muses assume the role of the Eumenides. A young woman most penitently confessed to a friend of mine that an unholy desire to read the women's magazines was her besetting 'temptation'.

It is the existence of these literary Puritans that has deterred me from applying the word *serious* to the right sort of readers and reading. It suggests

[1] I owe this characterisation of Racine to Mr Owen Barfield.

itself at first as just the word we want. But it is fatally equivocal. It may mean, on the one hand, something like 'grave' or 'solemn'; on the other, something more like 'thoroughgoing, whole-hearted, energetic'. Thus we say that Smith is 'a serious man', meaning that he is the reverse of gay, and that Wilson is 'a serious student', meaning that he studies hard. The serious man, far from being a serious student, may be a dabbler and a *dilettante*. The serious student may be as playful as Mercutio. A thing may be done seriously in the one sense and yet not in the other. The man who plays football for his health is a serious man: but no real footballer will call him a serious player. He is not whole-hearted about the game; doesn't really care. His seriousness as a man indeed involves his frivolity as a player; he only 'plays at playing', pretends to play. Now the true reader reads every work seriously in the sense that he reads it whole-heartedly, makes himself as receptive as he can. But for that very reason he cannot possibly read every work solemnly or gravely. For he will read 'in the same spirit that the author writ'. What is meant lightly he will take lightly; what is meant gravely, gravely. He will 'laugh and shake in Rabelais' easy chair' while he reads Chaucer's *faibliaux* and respond with exquisite frivolity to *The Rape of the Lock*. He will enjoy a kickshaw as a kickshaw and a tragedy as a tragedy. He will never commit the error of trying to munch whipped cream as if it were venison.

This is where the literary Puritans may fail most lamentably. They are too serious as men to be seriously receptive as readers. I have listened to an undergraduate's paper on Jane Austen from which, if I had not read them, I should never have discovered that there was the least hint of comedy in her novels. After a lecture of my own I have been accompanied from Mill Lane to Magdalene by a young man protesting with real anguish and horror against my wounding, my vulgar, my irreverent, suggestion that *The Miller's Tale* was written to make people laugh. And I have heard of another who finds *Twelfth Night* a penetrating study of the individual's relation to society. We are breeding up a race of young people who are as solemn as the brutes ('smiles from reason flow'); as solemn as a nineteen-year-old Scottish son of the manse at an English sherry party who takes all the compliments for declarations and all the banter for insult. Solemn men, but not serious readers; they have not fairly and squarely laid their minds open, without pre-conception, to the works they read.

Can we then, since all else fails, characterise the literary 'few' as *mature* readers? There will certainly be this much truth in the adjective; that excellence in our response to books, like excellence in other things, cannot be had without experience and discipline, and therefore cannot be had by the very young. But some of the truth still escapes us. If we are suggesting that all men naturally begin by treating literature like the many, and that all who, in their general psychology, succeed in becoming mature will also learn to read like the few, I believe we are wrong. I think the two kinds of readers are already foreshadowed in the nursery. Before they can read at all, while literature comes before them as stories not read but listened to, do not children react to it differently? Certainly, as soon as they can read for themselves, the two groups are already divided. There are those who read only when there is nothing better to do, gobble up each story to 'find out what happened', and seldom go back to it; others who reread and are profoundly moved.

All these attempts to characterise the two sorts of reader are, as I have said, hasty. I have mentioned them to get them out of the way. We must attempt to enter for ourselves into the attitudes involved. This ought to be possible for most of us because most of us, with respect to some of the arts, have passed from one to the other. We know something about the experience of the many not only from observation but from within.

III

HOW THE FEW AND THE MANY
USE PICTURES AND MUSIC

I GREW up in a place where there were no good pictures to see, so that my earliest acquaintance with the draughtsman's or the painter's art was wholly through the illustrations to books. Those to Beatrix Potter's *Tales* were the delight of my childhood; Arthur Rackham's to *The Ring*, that of my schooldays. I have all these books still. When I now turn their pages I by no means say 'How did I ever enjoy such bad work?' What surprises me is that I drew no distinctions in a collection where the work varied so vastly in merit. It now stares me in the face that in some of Beatrix Potter's plates you find witty drawing and pure colour, while others are ugly, ill-composed, and even perfunctory. (The classic economy and finality of her writing is far more evenly maintained.) In Rackham I now see admirable skies, trees, and grotesques, but observe that the human figures are often like dummies. How could I ever have failed to see this? I believe I can remember accurately enough to give the answer.

I liked Beatrix Potter's illustrations at a time when the idea of humanised animals fascinated me perhaps even more than it fascinates most children;

and I liked Rackham's at a time when Norse mythology was the chief interest of my life. Clearly, the pictures of both artists appealed to me because of what was represented. They were substitutes. If (at one age) I could really have seen humanised animals or (at another) could really have seen Valkyries, I should greatly have preferred it. Similarly, I admired the picture of a landscape only if, and only because, it represented country such as I would have liked to walk through in reality. A little later I admired a picture of a woman only if, and only because, it represented a woman who would have attracted me if she were really present.

The result, as I now see, was that I attended very inadequately to what was actually before me. It mattered intensely what the picture was 'of'; hardly at all what the picture was. It acted almost as a hieroglyph. Once it had set my emotions and imagination to work on the things depicted, it had done what I wanted. Prolonged and careful observation of the picture itself was not necessary. It might even have hindered the subjective activity.

All the evidence suggests to me that my own experience of pictures then was very much what that of the majority always remains.

Nearly all those pictures which, in reproduction, are widely popular are of things which in one way or another would in reality please or amuse or excite or move those who admire them—*The Monarch of the Glen, The Old Shepherd's Chief Mourner*,

Bubbles; hunting scenes and battles; death-beds and dinner parties; children, dogs, cats, and kittens; pensive young women (draped) to arouse sentiment, and cheerful young women (less draped) to arouse appetite.

The approving comments which those who buy such pictures make on them are all of one sort: 'That's the loveliest face I ever saw'—'Notice the old man's Bible on the table'—'You can see they're all listening'—'What a beautiful old house!' The emphasis is on what may be called the narrative qualities of the picture. Line or colour (as such) or composition are hardly mentioned. The skill of the artist sometimes is ('Look at the way he's got the effect of the candlelight on the wine glasses'). But what is admired is the realism—even with an approximation to *trompe-l'œil*—and the difficulty, real or supposed, of producing it.

But all these comments, and nearly all attention to the picture, cease soon after it has been bought. It soon dies for its owners; becomes like the once-read novel for the corresponding class of reader. It has been used and its work is done.

This attitude, which was once my own, might almost be defined as 'using' pictures. While you retain this attitude you treat the picture—or rather a hasty and unconscious selection of elements in the picture—as a self-starter for certain imaginative and emotional activities of your own. In other words, you 'do things with it'. You don't lay yourself open to what it, by being in its totality precisely the thing it is, can do to you.

You are thus offering to the picture the treatment which would be exactly right for two other sorts of representational object; namely the ikon and the toy. (I am not here using the word *ikon* in the strict sense given it by the Eastern Church; I mean any representational object, whether in two dimensions or three, which is intended as an aid to devotion.)

A particular toy or a particular ikon may be itself a work of art, but that is logically accidental; its artistic merits will not make it a better toy or a better ikon. They may make it a worse one. For its purpose is, not to fix attention upon itself, but to stimulate and liberate certain activities in the child or the worshipper. The Teddy-bear exists in order that the child may endow it with imaginary life and personality and enter into a quasi-social relationship with it. That is what 'playing with it' means. The better this activity succeeds the less the actual appearance of the object will matter. Too close or prolonged attention to its changeless and expressionless face impedes the play. A crucifix exists in order to direct the worshipper's thought and affections to the Passion. It had better not have any excellencies, subtleties, or originalities which will fix attention upon itself. Hence devout people may, for this purpose, prefer the crudest and emptiest ikon. The emptier, the more permeable; and they want, as it were, to pass through the material image and go beyond. For the same reason it is often not the costliest and most lifelike toy that wins the child's love.

If this is how the many use pictures, we must reject at once the haughty notion that their use is always and necessarily a vulgar and silly one. It may or may not be. The subjective activities of which they make pictures the occasion may be on all sorts of levels. To one such spectator Tintoretto's *Three Graces* may be merely an assistance in prurient imagination; he has used it as pornography. To another, it may be the starting-point for a meditation on Greek myth which, in its own right, is of value. It might conceivably, in its own different way, lead to something as good as the picture itself. This may be what happened when Keats looked at a Grecian urn. If so, his use of the vase was admirable. But admirable in its own way; not admirable as an appreciation of ceramic art. The corresponding uses of pictures are extremely various and there is much to be said for many of them. There is only one thing we can say with confidence against all of them without exception: they are not essentially appreciations of pictures.

Real appreciation demands the opposite process. We must not let loose our own subjectivity upon the pictures and make them its vehicles. We must begin by laying aside as completely as we can all our own preconceptions, interests, and associations. We must make room for Botticelli's Mars and Venus, or Cimabue's Crucifixion, by emptying out our own. After the negative effort, the positive. We must use our eyes. We must look, and go on looking till we have certainly seen exactly what is there. We sit down before the picture in order to have something done to us, not that we may do things with it. The first demand any work of any art makes upon us is surrender. Look. Listen. Receive. Get yourself out of the way. (There is no good asking first whether the work before you deserves such a surrender, for until you have surrendered you cannot possibly find out.)

It is not only our own 'ideas' about, say, Mars and Venus which must be set aside. That will make room only for Botticelli's 'ideas', in the same sense of the word. We shall thus receive only those elements in his invention which he shares with the poet. And since he is after all a painter and not a poet, this is inadequate. What we must receive is his specifically pictorial invention: that which makes out of many masses, colours, and lines the complex harmony of the whole canvas.

The distinction can hardly be better expressed than by saying that the many *use* art and the few *receive* it. The many behave in this like a man who talks when he should listen or gives when he should take. I do not mean by this that the right spectator is passive. His also is an imaginative activity; but an obedient one. He seems passive at first because he is making sure of his orders. If, when they have been fully grasped, he decides that they are not worth obeying—in other words, that this is a bad picture—he turns away altogether.

From the example of the man who uses Tintoretto as pornography it is apparent that a good work of art may be used in the wrong way. But it will seldom yield to this treatment so easily as a bad one. Such a man will gladly turn from Tintoretto to Kirchner or photographs if no moral or cultural hypocrisy prevents him. They contain fewer irrelevancies; more ham and less frill.

But the reverse is, I believe, impossible. A bad picture cannot be enjoyed with that full and disciplined 'reception' which the few give to a good one. This was borne in upon me lately when I was waiting at a bus stop near a hoarding and found myself, for a minute or so, really looking at a poster—a picture of a man and a girl drinking beer in a public house. It would not endure the treatment. Whatever merits it had seemed to have at the first glance diminished with every second of attention. The smiles became waxwork grins. The colour was, or seemed to me, tolerably realistic, but it was in no way delightful. There was nothing in the composition to satisfy the eye. The whole poster, besides being 'of' something, was not also a pleasing *object*. And this, I think, is what must happen to any bad picture if it is really examined.

If so, it is inaccurate to say that the majority 'enjoy bad pictures'. They enjoy the ideas suggested to them by bad pictures. They do not really see the pictures as they are. If they did, they could not live with them. There is a sense in which bad work never is nor can be enjoyed by anyone. The people do not like the bad picture *because* the faces in them are like those of puppets and there is no real mobility in the lines that are meant to be moving and no energy or grace in the whole design. These faults are simply invisible to them; as the actual face of the Teddy-bear is invisible to an imaginative and warm-hearted child when it is absorbed in its play. It no longer notices that the eyes are only beads.

If bad taste in art means a taste for badness as such, I have still to be convinced that any such thing exists. We assume that it does because we apply to all these popular enjoyments in the gross the adjective 'sentimental'. If we mean by this that they consist in the activity of what might be called 'sentiments', then (though I think some better word might be found) we are not far wrong. If we mean that these activities are all alike mawkish, flaccid, unreasonable, and generally disreputable, that is more than we know. To be moved by the thought of a solitary old shepherd's death and the fidelity of his dog is, in itself and apart from the present topic, not in the least a sign of inferiority. The real objection to that way of enjoying pictures is that you never get beyond yourself. The picture, so used, can call out of you only what is already there. You do not cross the frontier into that new region which the pictorial art as such has added to the world. *Zum Eckel find' ich immer nur mich.*

In music I suppose that most of us, perhaps nearly all of us, began life in the ranks of the many. In every performance of every work we attended exclusively to the 'tune'; to just so much of the total sound as could be represented by whistling or humming. Once this was grasped, all else became practically inaudible. One did not notice either how the composer treated it or how the performers rendered his treatment. To the tune itself there was, I believe, a twofold response.

First, and most obviously, a social and organic response. One wanted to 'join in'; to sing, to hum, to beat time, to sway one's body rhythmically. How often the many feel and indulge this impulse we all know only too well.

Secondly, there was an emotional response. We became heroic, lugubrious, or gay as the tune seemed to invite us. There are reasons for this cautious word 'seemed'. Some musical purists have told me that the appropriateness of certain airs to certain emotions is an illusion; certainly that it decreases with every advance in real musical understanding. It is by no means universal. Even in Eastern Europe the minor key has not the significance it has for most Englishmen; and when I heard a Zulu war song it sounded to me so wistful and gentle as to suggest a *berceuse* rather than the advance of a bloodthirsty impi. Sometimes, too, such emotional responses are dictated quite as much by the fanciful verbal titles which have been attached to certain compositions as by the music itself.

Once the emotional response is well aroused it begets imaginings. Dim ideas of inconsolable sorrows, brilliant revelry, or well-fought fields, arise. Increasingly it is these that we really enjoy. The very tune itself, let alone the use the composer makes of it and the quality of the performance, almost sinks out of hearing. As regards one instrument (the bagpipes) I am still in this condition. I can't tell one piece from another, nor a good piper from a bad. It is all just 'pipes', all equally intoxicating, heartrending, orgiastic. Boswell reacted thus to all music. 'I told him that it affected me to such a degree, as often to agitate my nerves painfully, producing in my mind alternate sensations of pathetic dejection, so that I was ready to shed tears, and of daring resolution, so that I was inclined to rush into the thickest part of the battle.' Johnson's reply will be remembered: 'Sir, I should never hear it, if it made me such a fool.'[1]

We have had to remind ourselves that the popular use of pictures, though not an appreciation of the pictures as they really are, need not be—though of course it very often is—base or degraded in itself. We hardly need a similar reminder about the popular use of music. A wholesale condemnation either of this organic, or this emotional response is out of

[1] Boswell, *Life of Johnson*, 23 September 1777.

the question. It could be made only in defiance of the whole human race. To sing and dance round a fiddler at a fair (the organic and social response) is obviously a right-minded thing to do. To have 'the salt tear harped out of your eye' is not foolish or shameful. And neither response is peculiar to the unmusical. The *cognoscenti* too can be caught humming or whistling. They too, or some of them, respond to the emotional suggestions of music.

But they don't hum or whistle while the music is going on; only in reminiscence, as we quote favourite lines of verse to ourselves. And the direct emotional impact of this or that passage is of very minor importance. When they have grasped the structure of the whole work, have received into their aural imagination the composer's (at once sensuous and intellectual) invention, they may have an emotion about that. It is a different sort of emotion and towards a different sort of object. It is impregnated with intelligence. Yet it is also far more sensuous than the popular use; more tied to the ear. They attend fully to the actual sounds that are being made. But of music as of pictures, the majority make a selection or précis, picking out the elements they can use and neglecting the rest. As the first demand of the picture is 'Look', the first demand of the music is 'Listen'. The composer may begin by giving out a 'tune' which you could whistle. But the question is not whether you particularly like that tune. Wait. Attend. See what he is going to make of it.

Yet I find a difficulty about music that I did not find about pictures. I cannot, however I try, rid myself of the feeling that some simple airs, quite apart from what is done with them and quite apart from the execution, are intrinsically vile and ugly. Certain popular songs and hymns come to mind. If my feeling is well-grounded, then it would follow that in music there can be bad taste in the positive sense; a delight in badness as such just because it is bad. But perhaps this means that I am not sufficiently musical. Perhaps the emotional invitation of certain airs to vulgar swagger or lacrimose self-pity so overpowers me that I cannot hear them as neutral patterns of which a good use might possibly be made. I leave it to true musicians to say whether there is no tune so odious (not even *Home sweet home*) that a great composer might not successfully make it one of the materials of a good symphony.

Fortunately the question can be left unanswered. In general the parallel between the popular uses of music and of pictures is close enough. Both consist of 'using' rather than 'receiving'. Both rush hastily forward to do things with the work of art instead of waiting for it to do something to them. As a result, a very great deal that is really visible on the canvas or audible in the performance is ignored; ignored because it cannot be so 'used'. And if the work contains nothing that can be so used—if there are no catchy tunes in the symphony, if the picture is of things that the majority does not care

25

about—it is completely rejected. Neither reaction need be in itself reprehensible; but both leave a man outside the full experience of the arts in question.

In both, when young people are just beginning to pass from the ranks of the many to those of the few, a ludicrous, but fortunately transient error may occur. The young person who has only recently discovered that there is in music something far more lastingly delightful than catchy tunes may go through a phase in which the mere occurrence of such a tune in any work makes him disdain it as 'cheap'. And another young man, at the same stage, may disdain as 'sentimental' any picture whose subject makes a ready appeal to the normal affections of the human mind. It is as if, having once discovered that there are other things to be demanded of a house than comfort, you then concluded that no comfortable house could be 'good architecture'.

I have said this error is transient. I meant transient in real lovers of music or of painting. But in status seekers and devotees of culture it may sometimes become a fixation.

IV

THE READING OF THE
UNLITERARY

WE can easily contrast the purely musical appreciation of a symphony with that of listeners to whom it is primarily or solely the starting-point for things so inaudible (and therefore non-musical) as emotions and visual images. But there can never be, in the same sense, a purely literary appreciation of literature. Every piece of literature is a sequence of words; and sounds (or their graphic equivalent) are words precisely because they carry the mind beyond themselves. That is what being a word means. To be carried mentally through and beyond musical sounds into something inaudible and non-musical may be the wrong way of treating music. But to be similarly carried through and beyond words into something non-verbal and non-literary is not a wrong way of reading. It is simply reading. Otherwise we should say we were reading when we let our eyes travel over the pages of a book in an unknown language, and we should be able to read the French poets without learning French. The first note of a symphony demands attention to nothing but itself. The first word of the *Iliad* directs our

27

minds to anger; something we are acquainted with outside the poem and outside literature altogether.

I am not here trying to prejudge the issue between those who say, and those who deny, that 'a poem should not mean but be'. Whatever is true of the poem, it is quite clear that the words in it must mean. A word which simply 'was' and didn't 'mean' would not be a word. This applies even to Nonsense poetry. *Boojum* in its context is not a mere noise. Gertrude Stein's 'a rose is a rose' if we thought it was 'arose is arose', would be different.

Every art is itself and not some other art. Every general principle we reach must, therefore, have a peculiar mode of application to each of the arts. Our next business is to discover the appropriate mode in which our distinction between using and receiving applies to reading. What, in the unliterary reader, corresponds to the unmusical listener's exclusive concentration on the 'top tune' and the use he makes of it? Our clue is the behaviour of such readers. It seems to me to have five characteristics.

1. They never, uncompelled, read anything that is not narrative. I do not mean that they all read fiction. The most unliterary reader of all sticks to 'the news'. He reads daily, with unwearied relish, how, in some place he has never seen, under circumstances which never become quite clear, someone he doesn't know has married, rescued, robbed, raped, or murdered someone else he doesn't know.

28

But this makes no essential difference between him and the class next above—those who read the lowest kinds of fiction. He wants to read about the same sorts of event as they. The difference is that, like Shakespeare's Mopsa, he wants to 'be sure they are true'. This is because he is so very unliterary that he can hardly think of invention as a legitimate, or even a possible activity. (The history of criticism shows that it took centuries to get Europe as a whole over this stile.)

2. They have no ears. They read exclusively by eye. The most horrible cacophonies and the most perfect specimens of rhythm and vocalic melody are to them exactly equal. It is by this that we discover some highly educated people to be un-literary. They will write 'the relation between mechanisation and nationalisation' without turning a hair.

3. Not only as regards the ear but also in every other way they are either quite unconscious of style, or even prefer books which we should think badly written. Offer an unliterary twelve-year-old (not all twelve-year-olds are unliterary) *Treasure Island* instead of the Boys' Bloods about pirates which are his usual fare, or offer Wells's *First Men in the Moon* to a reader of the infimal sorts of science fiction. You will often be disappointed. You give them, it would seem, just the sort of matter they want, but all far better done: descriptions that really describe, dialogue that can produce some illusion, characters

29

one can distinctly imagine. They peck about at it and presently lay the book aside. There is something in it that has put them off.

4. They enjoy narratives in which the verbal element is reduced to the minimum—'strip' stories told in pictures, or films with the least possible dialogue.

5. They demand swift-moving narrative. Something must always be 'happening'. Their favourite terms of condemnation are 'slow', 'long-winded', and the like.

It is not hard to see the common source of these characteristics. As the unmusical listener wants only the Tune, so the unliterary reader wants only the Event. The one ignores nearly all the sounds the orchestra is actually making; he wants to hum the tune. The other ignores nearly all that the words before him are doing; he wants to know what happened next.

He reads only narrative because only there will he find an Event. He is deaf to the aural side of what he reads because rhythm and melody do not help him to discover who married (rescued, robbed, raped or murdered) whom. He likes 'strip' narratives and almost wordless films because in them nothing stands between him and the Event. And he likes speed because a very swift story is all events.

His preferences in style need a little more consideration. It looks as if we had here met a liking for badness as such, for badness because it is bad. But I believe it is not so.

Our own judgement of a man's style, word by word and phrase by phrase, seems to us to be instantaneous; but it must always in reality be subsequent, by however infinitesimal an interval, to the effect the words and phrases have on us. Reading in Milton 'chequered shade' we find ourselves imagining a certain distribution of lights and shadows with unusual vividness, ease, and pleasure. We therefore conclude that 'chequered shade' is good writing. The result proves the excellence of the means. The clarity of the object proves that the lens we saw it through is good. Or we read that passage in *Guy Mannering*[1] where the hero looks at the sky and sees the planets each 'rolling' in its 'liquid orbit of light'. The image of planets visibly rolling or of visible orbits is so ludicrous that we do not even attempt to form it. Even if *orbits* is a blunder for 'orbs' we do not fare much better, for planets to the naked eye are not orbs nor even discs. We are presented with nothing but confusion. We therefore say that Scott was writing badly. This was a bad lens because we couldn't see through it. Similarly, from every sentence we read, our inner ear receives satisfaction or the reverse. On the strength of this experience we pronounce the author's rhythm to be good or bad.

It will be seen that all the experiences on which

[1] Cap. 3, *ad fin.*

our judgements are based depend on taking the words seriously. Unless we are fully attending both to sound and sense, unless we hold ourselves obediently ready to conceive, imagine, and feel as the words invite us, we shall not have these experiences. Unless you are really trying to look through the lens you cannot discover whether it is good or bad. We can never know that a piece of writing is bad unless we have begun by trying to read it as if it was very good and ended by discovering that we were paying the author an undeserved compliment. But the unliterary reader never intends to give the words more than the bare minimum of attention necessary for extracting the Event. Most of the things which good writing gives or bad writing fails to give are things he does not want and has no use for.

This explains why he does not value good writing. But it also explains why he prefers bad writing. In the picture stories of the 'strips' really good drawing is not only not demanded but would be an impediment. For every person or object must be instantly and effortlessly recognisable. The pictures are not there to be fully looked at but to be understood as statements; they are only one degree removed from hieroglyphics. Now words, for the unliterary reader, are in much the same position. The hackneyed *cliché* for every appearance or emotion (emotions may be part of the Event) is for him the best because it is immediately recognisable. 'My blood ran cold' is a hieroglyph for fear. Any attempt, such as a great writer might make, to render *this* fear concrete in its full particularity, is doubly a chokepear to the unliterary reader. For it offers him what he doesn't want, and offers it only on condition of his giving to the words a kind and degree of attention which he does not intend to give. It is like trying to sell him something he has no use for at a price he does not wish to pay.

Good writing may offend him by being either too spare for his purpose or too full. A woodland scene by D. H. Lawrence or a mountain valley by Ruskin gives him far more than he knows what to do with; on the other hand, he would be dissatisfied with Malory's 'he arrived afore a castle which was rich and fair and there was a postern opened towards the sea, and was open without any keeping, save two lions kept the entry, and the moon shone clear'.[1] Nor would he be content with 'I was terribly afraid' instead of 'My blood ran cold'. To the good reader's imagination such statements of the bare facts are often the most evocative of all. But the moon shining clear is not enough for the unliterary. They would rather be told that the castle was 'bathed in a flood of silver moonlight'. This is partly because their attention to the words they read is so insufficient. Everything has to be stressed, or 'written up', or it will barely be noticed. But still more, they want the hieroglyph—something that

[1] Caxton, XVII, 14 (Vinaver, 1014).

will release their stereotyped reactions to moonlight (moonlight, of course, as something in books, songs, and films; I believe that memories of the real world are very feebly operative while they read). Their way of reading is thus doubly and paradoxically defective. They lack the attentive and obedient imagination which would enable them to make use of any full and precise description of a scene or an emotion. On the other hand, they lack the fertile imagination which can build (in a moment) on the bare facts. What they therefore demand is a decent pretence of description and analysis, not to be read with care but sufficient to give them the feeling that the action is not going on in a vacuum—a few vague references to trees, shade and grass for a wood, or some allusion to popping corks and 'groaning tables' for a banquet. For this purpose, the more *clichés* the better. Such passages are to them what the backcloth is to most theatregoers. No one is going to pay any real attention to it, but everyone would notice its absence it it weren't there. Thus good writing, in one way or the other, nearly always offends the unliterary reader. When a good writer leads you into a garden he either gives you a precise impression of that particular garden at that particular moment—it need not be long, selection is what counts—or simply says 'It was in the garden, early'. The unliterary are pleased with neither. They call the first 'padding' and wish the author would 'cut the cackle and get to the horses'. The second they abhor as a vacuum; their imaginations cannot breathe in it.

Having said that the unliterary reader attends to the words too little to make anything like a full use of them, I must notice that there is another sort of reader who attends to them far too much and in the wrong way. I am thinking of what I call Style-mongers. On taking up a book, these people concentrate on what they call its 'style' or its 'English'. They judge this neither by its sound nor by its power to communicate but by its conformity to certain arbitrary rules. Their reading is a perpetual witch hunt for Americanisms, Gallicisms, split infinitives, and sentences that end with a preposition. They do not inquire whether the Americanism or Gallicism in question increases or impoverishes the expressiveness of our language. It is nothing to them that the best English speakers and writers have been ending sentences with prepositions for over a thousand years. They are full of arbitrary dislikes for particular words. One is 'a word they've always hated'; another 'always makes them think of so-and-so'. This is too common, and that too rare. Such people are of all men least qualified to have any opinion about a style at all; for the only two tests that are really relevant—the degree in which it is (as Dryden would say) 'sounding and significant'—are the two they never apply. They judge the instrument by anything rather than its power to do the work it was made for; treat language

35

as something that 'is' but does not 'mean'; criticise the lens after looking *at* it instead of *through* it. It was often said that the law about literary obscenity operated almost exclusively against particular words, that books were banned not for their tendency but for their vocabulary and a man could freely administer the strongest possible aphrodisiacs to his public provided he had the skill—and what competent writer has not?—to avoid the forbidden syllables. The Stylemonger's criteria, though for a different reason, are as wide of the mark as those of the law, and in the same way. If the mass of the people are unliterary, he is antiliterary. He creates in the minds of the unliterary (who have often suffered under him at school) a hatred of the very word *style* and a profound distrust of every book that is said to be well written. And if *style* meant what the Stylemonger values, this hatred and distrust would be right.

The unmusical, as I have said, pick out the Top Tune; and they use it for humming or whistling and for launching themselves upon emotional and imaginative reveries. The tunes they like best are of course those which lend themselves most easily to such uses. The unliterary similarly pick out the Event—'what happened'. The kinds of Event they like best and the uses they make of them go together. We can distinguish three main types.

They like what is called the 'exciting'—imminent dangers and hair-breadth escapes. The pleasure consists in the continual winding up and relaxing of (vicarious) anxiety. The existence of gamblers shows that even an actual anxiety gives many people pleasure, or is at least a necessary ingredient in a pleasurable whole. The popularity of helter-skelters and the like shows that the *sensations* of fear, when separated from a conviction of real danger, are pleasurable. Hardier spirits seek real danger and real fear for pleasure's sake; a mountain climber once said to me 'A climb is no fun unless there has been one moment at which you have sworn that if once you get down alive you will never go up a mountain again'. There is no mystery about the un-literary man's desire for 'excitement'. We all share it. We all like to watch a race with a close finish.

Secondly, they like to have inquisitiveness aroused, prolonged, exasperated, and finally satisfied. Hence the popularity of stories with a mystery in them. This pleasure is universal and needs no explanation. It makes a great part of the philosopher's, the scientist's, or the scholar's happiness. Also of the gossip's.

Thirdly, they like stories which enable them—vicariously, through the characters—to participate in pleasure or happiness. These are of various kinds. They may be love stories, and these may be either sensual and pornographic or sentimental and edifying. They may be success stories. They may be stories about high life, or simply about wealthy and luxurious life. We had better not assume that the vicarious delights, in any of these kinds, are always substitutes for actual delights. It is not only the plain and unloved women who read the love stories; all who read success stories are not themselves failures.

I distinguish the kinds thus for clarity. Actual books for the most part belong not wholly, but only predominantly, to one or other of them. The story of excitement or mystery usually has a 'love interest' tacked on to it, often perfunctorily. The love story or the idyll or High Life has to have some suspense and anxiety in it, however trivial these may be.

Let us be quite clear that the unliterary are unliterary not because they enjoy stories in these ways, but because they enjoy them in no other. Not what they have but what they lack cuts them off from the fulness of literary experience. These things ought they to have done and not left others undone. For all these enjoyments are shared by good readers reading good books. We hold our breath with anxiety while the Cyclops gropes over the ram that bears Odysseus, while we wonder how Phèdre (and Hippolyte) will react to the unexpected return of Thésée, or how the disgrace of the Bennet family will affect Darcy's love for Elizabeth. Our inquisitiveness is strongly excited by the first part of *The Confessions of a Justified Sinner* or the change in General Tilney's behaviour. We long to discover Pip's unknown benefactor in *Great Expectations*. In Spenser's House of Busirane every stanza whets our curiosity. As for the vicarious enjoyment of imagined happiness, the mere existence of the Pastoral gives it a respectable place in literature. And elsewhere too, though we do not demand a happy ending to every story, yet when such an ending occurs and is fitting and well executed, we certainly enjoy the happiness of the characters. We are even prepared to enjoy vicariously the fulfilment of utterly impossible wishes, as in the statue scene from the *Winter's Tale*; for what wish is so impossible as the wish that the dead to whom we have been cruel and unjust should live again and forgive us and 'all be as before'? Those who seek only vicarious happiness in their reading are unliterary; but those who pretend that it can never be an ingredient in good reading are wrong.

V

ON MYTH

BEFORE we go any further I must turn aside to remove a misapprehension which the last chapter may have invited.

Compare the following:

1. There was a man who sang and played the harp so well that even beasts and trees crowded to hear him. And when his wife died he went down alive into the land of the dead and made music before the King of the Dead till even he had compassion and gave him back his wife, on condition that he led her up out of that land without once looking back to see her until they came out into the light. But when they were nearly out, one moment too soon, the man looked back, and she vanished from him forever.

2. 'There was a man who was away from home for many years, for Poseidon kept a hostile eye on him, and all that time the suitors of his wife were wasting his property and plotting against his son. But he got home with much hardship, made himself known to a few, saved his own life, and killed his enemies.' (This is Aristotle's synopsis of the *Odyssey* in *Poetics* 1455[b].)

3. Let us suppose—for I certainly won't write it—a synopsis on the same scale of *Barchester Towers*, *Middlemarch*, or *Vanity Fair*; or of some much shorter work, like Wordsworth's *Michael*, Constant's *Adolphe* or *The Turn of the Screw*.

The first, though it is a bare outline, set down in the first words that come to hand, would, I believe, make a powerful impression on any person of sensibility, if he here met that story for the first time. The second is not nearly such satisfactory reading. We see that a good story could be written on this plot, but the abstract is not a good story itself. As for the third, the abstract I have not written, we see at once that it would be completely worthless—not only worthless as a representation of the book in question, but worthless in itself; dull beyond bearing, unreadable.

There is, then, a particular kind of story which has a value in itself—a value independent of its embodiment in any literary work. The story of Orpheus strikes and strikes deep, of itself; the fact that Virgil and others have told it in good poetry is irrelevant. To think about it and be moved by it is not necessarily to think about those poets or to be moved by them. It is true that such a story can hardly reach us except in words. But this is logically accidental. If some perfected art of mime or silent film or serial pictures could make it clear with no words at all, it would still affect us in the same way.

One might have expected that the plots of the crudest adventure stories, written for those who want only the Event, would have this extra-literary quality. But it is not so. You could not fob them off with a synopsis instead of the story itself. They want only the Event, but the Event will not reach them unless it is 'written up'. Moreover, their simplest stories are far too complicated for a readable

41

abstract; too many things happen. The stories I am thinking of always have a very simple narrative shape—a satisfactory and inevitable shape, like a good vase or a tulip.

It is difficult to give such stories any name except *myths*, but that word is in many ways unfortunate. In the first place we must remember that Greek *muthos* does not mean this sort of story but any sort of story. Secondly, not all stories which an anthropologist would classify as myths have the quality I am here concerned with. When we speak of myths, as when we speak of ballads, we are usually thinking of the best specimens and forgetting the majority. If we go steadily through all the myths of any people we shall be appalled by much of what we read. Most of them, whatever they may have meant to ancient or savage man, are to us meaningless and shocking; shocking not only by their cruelty and obscenity but by their apparent silliness—almost what seems insanity. Out of this rank and squalid undergrowth the great myths—Orpheus, Demeter and Persephone, the Hesperides, Balder, Ragnarok, or Ilmarinen's forging of the Sampo—rise like elms. Conversely, certain stories which are not myths in the anthropological sense, having been invented by individuals in fully civilised periods, have what I should call the 'mythical quality'. Such are the plots of *Dr Jekyll and Mr Hyde*, Wells's *The Door in the Wall* or Kafka's *The Castle*. Such is the conception of Gormenghast in Mr Peake's *Titus Groan* or of the Ents and Lothlorien in Professor Tolkien's *Lord of the Rings*.

In spite of these inconveniences I must either use the word *myth* or coin a word, and I think the former the lesser evil of the two. Those who read to understand—I make no provision for Stylemongers —will take the word in the sense I give it. A myth means, in this book, a story which has the following characteristics.

1. It is, in the sense I have already indicated, extra-literary. Those who have got at the same myth through Natalis Comes, Lemprière, Kingsley, Hawthorne, Robert Graves, or Roger Green, have a mythical experience in common; and it is important, not merely an H.C.F. In contrast to this, those who have got the same story from Brook's *Romeus* and Shakespeare's *Romeo* share a mere H.C.F., in itself valueless.

2. The pleasure of myth depends hardly at all on such usual narrative attractions as suspense or surprise. Even at a first hearing it is felt to be inevitable. And the first hearing is chiefly valuable in introducing us to a permanent object of contemplation— more like a thing than a narration—which works upon us by its peculiar flavour or quality, rather as a smell or a chord does. Sometimes, even from the first, there is hardly any narrative element. The idea that the gods, and all good men, live under the shadow of Ragnarok is hardly a story. The Hesperides, with their apple-tree and dragon, are already

43

a potent myth, without bringing in Herakles to steal the apples.

3. Human sympathy is at a minimum. We do not project ourselves at all strongly into the characters. They are like shapes moving in another world. We feel indeed that the pattern of their movements has a profound relevance to our own life, but we do not imaginatively transport ourselves into theirs. The story of Orpheus makes us sad; but we are sorry for all men rather than vividly sympathetic with him, as we are, say, with Chaucer's Troilus.

4. Myth is always, in one sense of that word, 'fantastic'. It deals with impossibles and preternaturals.

5. The experience may be sad or joyful but it is always grave. Comic myth (in my sense of *myth*) is impossible.

6. The experience is not only grave but awe-inspiring. We feel it to be numinous. It is as if something of great moment had been communicated to us. The recurrent efforts of the mind to grasp—we mean, chiefly, to conceptualise—this something, are seen in the persistent tendency of humanity to provide myths with allegorical explanations. And after all allegories have been tried, the myth itself continues to feel more important than they.

I am describing and not accounting for myths. To inquire how they arise—whether they are primitive science or the fossil remains of rituals, or the fabrications of medicine men, or outcroppings from

44

the individual or the collective unconscious—is quite outside my purpose. I am concerned with the effect of myths as they act on the conscious imagination of minds more or less like our own, not with their hypothetical effect on pre-logical minds or their pre-history in the unconscious. For it is only the former that can be directly observed or that brings the subject within hailing distance of literary studies. When I talk of dreams I mean, and can only mean, dreams as they are remembered after waking. Similarly, when I talk of myths I mean myths as we experience them: that is, myths contemplated but not believed, dissociated from ritual, held up before the fully waking imagination of a logical mind. I deal only with that part of the iceberg which shows above the surface; it alone has beauty, it alone exists as an object of contemplation. No doubt there is plenty down below. The desire to investigate the parts below has genuinely scientific justification. But the peculiar attraction of the study, I suspect, springs in part from the same impulse which makes men allegorise the myths. It is one more effort to seize, to conceptualise, the important something which the myth seems to suggest.

Since I define myths by their effect on us, it is plain that for me the same story may be a myth to one man and not to another. This would be a fatal defect if my aim were to provide criteria by which we can classify stories as mythical or non-mythical. But that is not my aim. I am concerned with ways of reading, and that is why this digression on myths has been necessary.

The man who first learns what is to him a great myth through a verbal account which is baldly or vulgarly or cacophonously written, discounts and ignores the bad writing and attends solely to the myth. He hardly minds about the writing. He is glad to have the myth on any terms. But this would seem to be almost exactly the same behaviour which, in the previous chapter, I attributed to the un-literary. In both there is the same minimum atten-tion to the words and the same concentration on the Event. Yet if we equated the lover of myth with the mass of the unliterary we should be deeply mistaken.

The difference is that, while both use the same procedure, he uses it where it is proper and fruitful and they do not. The value of myth is not a specifi-cally literary value, nor the appreciation of myth a specifically literary experience. He does not approach the words with the expectation or belief that they are good reading matter; they are merely information. Their literary merits or faults do not count (for his main purpose) much more than those of a timetable or a cookery book. Of course it may happen that the words which tell him the myth are themselves a work of fine literary art—as in the prose Edda. If he is a literary person—and he nearly always is—he will then delight in that literary work for its own sake. But this literary delight will be distinct from his appreciation of the myth; just as our pictorial enjoyment of Botticelli's Birth of Venus is distinct from our reactions, whatever they may be, to the myth it celebrates.

The unliterary, on the other hand, have sat down to 'read a book'. They have surrendered their imaginations to the guidance of an author. But it is a half-hearted surrender. They can do very little for themselves. Everything has to be stressed, written up, and clothed in the right *clichés*, if it is to hold their attention. But at the same time they have no notion of strict obedience to the words. Their behaviour is in one way more literary than that of the man who seeks, and loves, a myth through the dry summary in a classical dictionary; more literary because it is bounded by, wholly dependent on, the book. But it is also so hazy and hasty that it could use hardly anything of what a good book offers. They are like those pupils who want to have everything explained to them and do not much attend to the explanation. And though, like the myth-lover, they concentrate on the Event, it is a very different kind of Event and a very different kind of concentration. He will be moved by the myth as long as he lives; they, when the momentary excitement is over and the momentary curiosity appeased, will forget the Event forever. And rightly, for the sort of Event they value has no claims on the lasting allegiance of the imagination.

In a word, the behaviour of the myth-lover is

extra-literary, while theirs is unliterary. He gets
out of myths what myths have to give. They do not
get out of reading one-tenth or one-fiftieth of what
reading has to give.

As I have already said, the degree to which any
story is a myth depends very largely on the person
who hears or reads it. An important corollary
follows. We must never assume[1] that we know
exactly what is happening when anyone else reads
a book. For beyond all doubt the same book can be
merely an exciting 'yarn' to one and convey a myth,
or something like a myth, to another. The reading of
Rider Haggard is especially ambiguous in this respect.
If you find two boys both reading his romances
you must not conclude that they are having the
same experience. Where one finds only danger for
the heroes, the other may feel the 'aweful'. Where
one races ahead in curiosity, the other may pause in
wonder. For the unliterary boy the elephant-hunts
and shipwrecks may be just as good as the mythical
element—they are equally 'exciting'—and Haggard
in general may give just the same sort of entertainment as John Buchan. The myth-loving boy, if he
is also literary, will soon discover that Buchan is by
far the better writer; but he will still be aware of
reaching through Haggard something which is quite
incommensurable with mere excitement. Reading
Buchan, he asks 'Will the hero escape?' Reading
Haggard, he feels 'I shall never escape this. This

[1] I do not say we can never find out.

will never escape me. These images have struck roots far below the surface of my mind.'

The similarity of method between reading for the myth and the characteristic reading of the un-literary is thus superficial. And they are practised by different sorts of people. I have met literary people who had no taste for myth, but I have never met an unliterary person who had it. The unliterary will accept stories which we judge to be grossly improbable; their psychology, the state of society depicted, the turns of fortune, are incredible. But they will not accept admitted impossibles and preter-naturals. 'It couldn't really happen', they say, and put the book down. They think it 'silly'. Thus while something we could call 'fantasy' makes a very great part of their experience as readers, they invariably dislike the fantastic. But this distinction warns me that we cannot penetrate much further into their preferences without defining terms.

VI

THE MEANINGS OF 'FANTASY'

THE word *fantasy* is both a literary and a psychological term. As a literary term a fantasy means any narrative that deals with impossibles and preternaturals. *The Ancient Mariner*, *Gulliver*, *Erewhon*, *The Wind in the Willows*, *The Witch of Atlas*, *Jurgen*, *The Crock of Gold*, the *Vera Historia*, *Micromegas*, *Flatland* and Apuleius' *Metamorphoses* are fantasies. Of course they are very heterogeneous in spirit and purpose. The only thing common to them is the fantastic. I shall call this sort of fantasy 'literary fantasy'.

As a psychological term *fantasy* has three meanings.

1. An imaginative construction which in some way or other pleases the patient and is mistaken by him for reality. A woman in this condition imagines that some famous person is in love with her. A man believes that he is the long-lost son of noble and wealthy parents and that he will soon be discovered, acknowledged, and overwhelmed with luxuries and honours. The commonest events are twisted, often not without ingenuity, into evidence for the treasured belief. To this kind of fantasy I need give no name because we need not mention it again.

Delusion, except by some accident, is of no literary interest.

2. A pleasing imaginative construction entertained incessantly, and to his injury, by the patient, but without the delusion that it is a reality. A waking dream—known to be such by the dreamer—of military or erotic triumphs, of power or grandeur, even of mere popularity, is either monotonously reiterated or elaborated year by year. It becomes the prime consolation, and almost the only pleasure, of the dreamer's life. Into 'this invisible riot of the mind, this secret prodigality of being' he retires whenever the necessities of life set him free. Realities, even such realities as please other men, grow insipid to him. He becomes incapable of all the efforts needed to achieve a happiness not merely notional. The dreamer about limitless wealth will not save sixpence. The imaginary Don Juan will take no pains to make himself ordinarily agreeable to any woman he meets. I call this activity Morbid Castle-building.

3. The same activity indulged in moderately and briefly as a temporary holiday or recreation, duly subordinated to more effective and outgoing activities. Whether a man would be wiser to live with none of this at all in his life, we need not perhaps discuss, for no one does. Nor does such reverie always end in itself. What we actually do is often what we dreamed of doing. The books we write were once books which, in a day-dream, we pictured

51

ourselves writing—though of course never quite so perfect. I call this Normal Castle-building.

But normal castle-building itself can be of two kinds and the difference between them is all-important. They may be called the Egoistic and the Disinterested. In the first kind the day-dreamer himself is always the hero and everything is seen through his eyes. It is he who makes the witty retorts, captivates the beautiful women, owns the ocean-going yacht, or is acclaimed as the greatest living poet. In the other kind, the day-dreamer is not the hero of the day-dream or perhaps not present in it at all. Thus a man who has no chance of going to Switzerland in reality may entertain himself with reveries about an Alpine holiday. He will be present in the fiction, but not as hero; rather as spectator. As his attention would be fixed not on himself but on the mountains if he were really in Switzerland, so in the castle-building his attention is fixed on the imagined mountains. But sometimes the dreamer is not present in the day-dream at all. I am probably one of many who, on a wakeful night, entertain themselves with invented landscapes. I trace great rivers from where the gulls scream at the estuary, through the windings of ever narrower and more precipitous gorges, up to the barely audible tinkling of their source in a fold of the moors. But I am not there myself as explorer or even as tourist. I am looking at that world from outside. A further stage is often reached by children, usually in co-operation. They may feign a whole world and people it and remain outside it. But when that stage is reached, something more than mere reverie has come into action: construction, invention, in a word *fiction*, is proceeding.

There is thus, if the day-dreamer has any talent, an easy transition from disinterested castle-building to literary invention. There is even a transition from Egoistic to Disinterested and thence to genuine fiction. Trollope tells us in his autobiography how his own novels thus grew out of castle-building which had originally been of the most flagrantly egoistic and compensatory type.

In the present inquiry, however, we are concerned not with the relation between castle-building and composition but with that between castle-building and reading. I have already said that one kind of story dear to the unliterary is that which enables them to enjoy love or wealth or distinction vicariously through the characters. It is in fact guided or conducted egoistic castle-building. While they read they project themselves into the most enviable or most admirable character; and probably, after they have finished reading, his delights and victories supply hints for further day-dreams.

It is sometimes, I think, assumed that all the reading of the unliterary is of this sort and involves this projection. By '*this* projection' I mean a projection for the sake of vicarious pleasures, triumphs, and distinctions. Some sort of projection into all the major characters, villains as well as heroes, enviable and pitiable alike, is no doubt necessary for all readers of all stories. We must 'empathise', must enter into their feelings, or we might as well read about the loves of the triangles. But it would be rash to assume that even for unliterary readers of popular fiction there is always a projection of the egoistic castle-builder's type.

For one thing, some of them like comic stories. I do not think that the enjoyment of a joke is ever, for them or for anyone else, a form of castle-building. We certainly do not wish to *be* the cross-gartered Malvolio or Mr Pickwick in the pond. We might conceivably say 'I wish I'd been there to see'; but this is only to wish ourselves as spectators—which we already are—in what we suppose to be a better seat. Again, many of the unliterary like stories of ghosts and other horrors; but the better they like them the less they would wish to be characters in one themselves. It is possible that stories of adventures are sometimes enjoyed because the reader sees himself in the role of the courageous and resourceful hero. But I do not think we can be sure that this is always the only or even the main pleasure. He may admire such a hero and desire his success without making that success his own.

There remains a residue of stories whose attraction, as far as we can see, can depend on nothing but egoistic castle-building; success stories, certain love stories, and certain stories of high life. These are the favourite reading of readers in the lowest class; lowest, because reading takes them least out of themselves, confirms them in an indulgence which they already use too much, and turns them away from most of what is most worth having both in books and life. This castle-building, whether done with the aid of books or unaided, is what the psychologists call fantasy, in one of its senses. If we had not made the necessary distinctions it would, therefore, be easy to assume that such readers would like literary fantasies. The reverse is true. Make experiments and you will find that they detest them; think them 'only fit for kids', see no point in reading about 'things that could never really happen'.

To us it is apparent that the books they like are full of impossibilities. They have no objection to monstrous psychology and preposterous coincidence. But they demand rigorously an observance of such natural laws as they know and a general ordinariness; the clothes, gadgets, food, houses, occupations, and tone of the everyday world. This is, no doubt, partly due to the extreme inertia of their imaginations. They can render real to themselves only what they have read of a thousand times and seen a hundred times before. But there is a deeper reason.

Though they do not mistake their castle-building for reality, they want to feel that it might be. The woman reader does not believe that all eyes follow her, as they follow the heroine of the book; but she wants to feel that, given more money, and therefore better dresses, jewels, cosmetics, and opportunities, they might. The man does not believe that he is rich and socially successful; but if only he won a sweepstake, if only fortunes could be made without talent, he might become so. He knows the daydream is unrealised; he demands that it should be, in principle, realisable. That is why the slightest hint of the admittedly impossible ruins his pleasure. A story which introduces the marvellous, the fantastic, says to him by implication 'I am merely a work of art. You must take me as such—must enjoy me for my suggestions, my beauty, my irony, my construction, and so forth. There is no question of anything like this happening to you in the real world.' After that, reading—his sort of reading—becomes pointless. Unless he can feel 'This might—who knows?—this might one day happen to me', the whole purpose for which he reads is frustrated. It is, therefore, an absolute rule: the more completely a man's reading is a form of egoistic castle-building, the more he will demand a certain superficial realism, and the less he will like the fantastic. He wishes to be deceived, at least momentarily, and nothing can deceive unless it bears a plausible resemblance to reality. Disinterested castle-building may dream of nectar and ambrosia, of fairy bread and honey dew; the egoistic sort dreams rather of bacon and eggs or steak.

But I have already used the word *realism* which is equivocal and must be taken to pieces.

VII

ON REALISMS

THE word *realism* has one meaning in logic, where its opposite is nominalism, and another in metaphysics, where its opposite is idealism. In political language it has a third and somewhat debased meaning; the attitudes we should call 'cynical' in our opponents are called 'realistic' when our own side adopts them. At present we are concerned with none of these, but only with *realism* and *realistic* as terms of literary criticism. And even within this restricted area a distinction must immediately be drawn.

We should all describe as realistic the exact specifications of size which are given by direct measurements in *Gulliver* or by comparison with well-known objects in the *Divine Comedy*. And when Chaucer's friar drives the cat off the bench where he wants to sit down himself, we should describe this as a realistic touch.[1] This is what I call Realism of Presentation—the art of bringing something close to us, making it palpable and vivid, by sharply observed or sharply imagined detail. We may cite as examples the dragon 'sniffing along the stone' in *Beowulf*; Layamon's Arthur, who, on hearing that

[1] *Canterbury Tales*, D. 1775.

57

he was king, sat very quiet and 'one time he was red and one time he was pale'; the pinnacles in *Gawain* that looked as if they were 'pared out of paper'; Jonah going into the whale's mouth 'like a mote at a minster door'; the fairy bakers in *Huon* rubbing the paste off their fingers; Falstaff on his death-bed plucking at the sheet; Wordsworth's little streams heard at evening but 'inaudible by daylight'.[1]

For Macaulay such realism of presentation was what chiefly distinguished Dante from Milton. And Macaulay was right so far as he went, but never realised that what he had stumbled on was not a difference between two particular poets but a general difference between medieval and classical work. The Middle Ages favoured a brilliant and exuberant development of presentational realism, because men were at that time inhibited neither by a sense of period—they dressed every story in the manners of their own day—nor by a sense of decorum. The medieval tradition gives us 'Fire and fleet and candle-light'; the classical, *C'était pendant l'horreur d'une profonde nuit.*

It will be noticed that most of my examples of presentational realism, though I did not select them for that purpose, occur in the telling of stories which are not themselves at all 'realistic' in the sense of being probable or even possible. This should clear up once and for all a very elementary confusion

[1] *Beowulf,* 2288; *Brut,* 1987 *sq.*; *Gawain and the Green Knight,* 802; *Patience,* 268; *Duke Huon of Burdeux,* II, cxvi, p. 409, ed. S. Lee, E.E.T.S.; *Henry V,* II, iii, 14; *Excursion,* IV, 1174.

which I have sometimes detected between realism of presentation and what I call realism of content.

A fiction is realistic in content when it is probable or 'true to life'. We see realism of content, isolated from the slightest realism of presentation and therefore 'chemically pure', in a work like Constant's *Adolphe*. There a passion, and the sort of passion that is not very rare in the real world, is pursued through all its windings to the death. There is no disbelief to be suspended. We never doubt that this is just what might happen. But while there is much to be felt and much to be analysed, there is nothing to be seen or heard or tasted or touched. There are no 'close-ups', no details. There are no minor characters and even no places worthy of the name. Except in one short passage, for a special purpose, there is no weather and no countryside. So in Racine, given the situation, all is probable, even inevitable. The realism of content is great, but there is no realism of presentation. We do not know what anyone looked like, or wore, or ate. Everyone speaks in the same style. There are almost no manners. I know very well what it would be like to *be* Oreste (or Adolphe); but I should not know either if I met him, as I should certainly know Pickwick or Falstaff, and probably old Karamazov or Bercilak.

The two realisms are quite independent. You can get that of presentation without that of content, as in medieval romance: or that of content without that of presentation, as in French (and some Greek) tragedy; or both together, as in *War and Peace*; or neither, as in the *Furioso* or *Rasselas* or *Candide*.

In this age it is important to remind ourselves that all four ways of writing are good and masterpieces can be produced in any of them. The dominant taste at present demands realism of content.[1] The great achievements of the nineteenth-century novel have trained us to appreciate and to expect it. But we should be making a disastrous mistake and creating one more false classification of books and readers if we erected this natural and historically conditioned preference into a principle. There is some danger of this. No one that I know of has indeed laid down in so many words that a fiction cannot be fit for adult and civilised reading unless it represents life as we have all found it to be, or probably shall find it to be, in experience. But some such assumption seems to lurk tacitly in the background of much criticism and literary discussion. We feel it in the widespread neglect or disparagement of the romantic, the idyllic, and the fantastic, and the readiness to stigmatise instances of these as 'escapism'. We feel it when books are praised for being 'comments on', or 'reflections' (or more deplorably 'slices') of Life. We notice also that 'truth to life' is held to have a claim on literature that overrides all other considerations.

[1] And usually realism of presentation as well. But the latter is not relevant at this point.

Authors, restrained by our laws against obscenity—rather silly laws, it may be—from using half a dozen monosyllables, felt as if they were martyrs of science, like Galileo. To the objection 'This is obscene' or 'This is depraved', or even to the more critically relevant objection 'This is uninteresting', the reply 'This occurs in real life' seems at times to be thought almost sufficient.

We must first decide what sort of fictions can justly be said to have truth to life. I suppose we ought to say that a book has this property when a sensible reader, on finishing it, can feel, 'Yes. This —thus grim, or splendid, or empty, or ironic—is what our life is like. This is the sort of thing that happens. This is how people behave.'

But when we say 'The sort of thing that happens', do we mean the sort of thing that usually or often happens, the sort of thing that is typical of the human lot? Or do we mean 'The sort of thing that might conceivably happen or that, by a thousandth chance, may have happened once'? For there is a great difference in this respect between the *Oedipus Tyrannus* or *Great Expectations* on the one hand and *Middlemarch* or *War and Peace* on the other. In the first two we see (by and large) such events and such behaviour as would be probable and characteristic of human life, given the situation. But the situation itself is not. It is extremely unlikely that a poor boy should be suddenly enriched by an anonymous benefactor who later turns out to be a convict. The chances against anyone's being exposed as an infant, then rescued, then adopted by a king, then by one coincidence killing his father, and then by another coincidence marrying his father's widow, are overwhelming. The bad luck of Oedipus calls for as much suspension of disbelief as the good luck of Monte Cristo.[1] In George Eliot's and Tolstoy's masterpieces, on the other hand, all is probable and typical of human life. These are the sort of things that might happen to anyone. Things like them have probably happened to thousands. These are such people as we might meet any day. We can say without reservation,'This is what life is like'.

Fictions of both these kinds may be distinguished from literary fantasies such as the *Furioso* or *The Ancient Mariner* or *Vathek*, but they should also be distinguished from each other. And as soon as we distinguish them we cannot help noticing that until quite modern times nearly all stories were of the first type—belonged to the family of the *Oedipus*, not to that of *Middlemarch*. Just as all except bores relate in conversation not what is normal but what is exceptional—you mention having seen a giraffe in Petty Cury, but don't mention having seen an undergraduate—so authors told of the exceptional. Earlier audiences would not have seen the point of a story about anything else. Faced with such matters as we get in *Middlemarch* or *Vanity Fair*

[1] See Appendix.

or *The Old Wives' Tale*, they would have said 'But this is all perfectly ordinary. This is what happens every day. If these people and their fortunes were so unremarkable, why are you telling us about them at all?' We can learn the world-wide and immemorial attitude of man to stories from noticing how stories are introduced in conversation. Men begin 'The strangest sight I ever saw was—', or 'I'll tell you something queerer even than that', or 'Here's something you'll hardly believe'. Such was the spirit of nearly all stories before the nineteenth century. The deeds of Achilles or Roland were told of because they were exceptionally and improbably heroic; the matricidal burden of Orestes, because it was an exceptional and improbable burden; the saint's life, because he was exceptionally and improbably holy. The bad luck of Oedipus, or Balin, or Kullervo, was told because it was beyond all precedent. The Reeve's Tale was told because what happens in it is unusually and all but impossibly funny.

Clearly, then, if we are such radical realists as to hold that all good fiction must have truth to life, we shall have to take one or other of two lines. On the one hand, we can say that the only good fictions are those which belong to the second type, the family of *Middlemarch*: fictions of which we can say without reservation 'Life is like this'. If we do that we shall have against us the literary practice and experience of nearly the whole human race. That is

too formidable an antagonist. *Securus judicat.*
Or else we shall have to argue that stories such
as that of Oedipus, stories of the exceptional and
atypical (and therefore remarkable) are also true
to life.

Well, if we are sufficiently determined, we can
just—only just—brazen it out. We can maintain
that such stories are implicitly saying 'Life is such
that even this is possible. A man might conceivably
be raised to affluence by a grateful convict. A man
might conceivably be as unlucky as Balin. A man
might conceivably get burned with a hot iron and
cry out "Water" just in time to induce a silly old
landlord to cut a rope because he had been pre-
viously persuaded that "Noe's flood" was coming
again. A city might conceivably be taken by a
wooden horse.' And we should have to maintain not
only that they are saying this, but that they say it
truly.

But even if all this were granted—and the last
item takes a good deal of swallowing—the position
would seem to me entirely artificial; something
thought up in defence of a desperate thesis and
quite out of tune with the experience we have when
we receive the stories. Even if the stories permit
the conclusion 'Life is such that this is possible',
can anyone believe that they invite it, that they are
told or heard for the sake of it, that it is anything
more than a remote accident? For those who tell the
story and those (including ourselves) who receive it

are not thinking about any such generality as human life. Attention is fixed on something concrete and individual; on the more than ordinary terror, splendour, wonder, pity, or absurdity of a particular case. These, not for any light they might throw hereafter on the life of man, but for their own sake, are what matters.

When such stories are well done we usually get what may be called hypothetical probability—what would be probable if the initial situation occurred. But the situation itself is usually treated as if it were immune from criticism. In simpler ages it is accepted on authority. Our ancestors have vouched for it; 'myn auctour' or 'thise olde wise'. It is regarded, if poets and audience raise the question at all, as we regard a historical fact. And fact, unlike fiction, if sufficiently well attested, does not need to be probable. Very often it is not. Sometimes we are even warned against drawing from the narrative any conclusion about life in general. When a hero lifts a great stone Homer tells us that no two modern men, no two men in the world of our experience, could move it.[1] Herakles, says Pindar, saw the land of the Hyperboreans; but don't imagine you'll ever get there.[2] In more sophisticated periods, the situation is accepted rather as a postulate. 'Let it be granted' that Lear divided his kingdom; that the 'riche gnof' in the *Miller's Tale* was infinitely gullible; that a girl who

[1] *Iliad*, v, 302 *sq.*   [2] *Olympian* iii, 31; *Pythian* x, 29 *sq.*

65

puts on boy's clothes becomes instantly unrecognisable to everyone, including her lover; that calumnies against our nearest and dearest, even when uttered by the most suspicious characters, will be believed. Surely the author is not saying 'This is the sort of thing that happens'? Or surely, if he is, he lies? But he is not. He is saying, 'Suppose this happened, how interesting, how moving, the consequences would be! Listen. It would be like this.' To question the postulate itself would show a misunderstanding; like asking why trumps should be trumps. It is the sort of thing Mopsa does. That is not the point. The *raison d'être* of the story is that we shall weep, or shudder, or wonder, or laugh as we follow it.

The effort to force such stories into a radically realistic theory of literature seems to me perverse. They are not, in any sense that matters, representations of life as we know it, and were never valued for being so. The strange events are not clothed with hypothetical probability in order to increase our knowledge of real life by showing how it would react to this improbable test. It is the other way round. The hypothetical probability is brought in to make the strange events more fully imaginable. Hamlet is not faced with a ghost in order that his reactions may tell us more about his nature and therefore about human nature in general; he is shown reacting naturally in order that we may accept the ghost. The demand that all literature should have realism of content cannot be maintained. Most of the great literature so far produced in the world has not. But there is a quite different demand which we can properly make; not that all books should be realistic in content, but that every book should have as much of this realism as it pretends to have.

This principle does not appear to be always understood. There are earnest people who recommend realistic reading for everyone because, they say, it prepares us for real life, and who would, if they could, forbid fairy-tales for children and romances for adults because these 'give a false picture of life' —in other words, deceive their readers.

I trust that what has already been said about egoistic castle-building forearms us against this error. Those who wish to be deceived always demand in what they read at least a superficial or apparent realism of content. To be sure, the show of such realism which deceives the mere castle-builder would not deceive a literary reader. If he is to be deceived, a much subtler and closer resemblance to real life will be required. But without some degree of realism in content—a degree proportional to the reader's intelligence—no deception will occur at all. No one can deceive you unless he makes you think he is telling the truth. The unblushingly romantic has far less power to deceive than the apparently realistic. Admitted fantasy is precisely the kind of literature which never deceives at all. Children are not deceived by fairy-tales; they are often and gravely deceived by school-stories. Adults are not deceived by science-fiction; they can be deceived by the stories in the women's magazines. None of us are deceived by the *Odyssey*, the *Kalevala*, *Beowulf*, or Malory. The real danger lurks in sober-faced novels where all appears to be very probable but all is in fact contrived to put across some social or ethical or religious or anti-religious 'comment on life'. For some at least of such comments must be false. To be sure, no novel will deceive the best type of reader. He never mistakes art either for life or for philosophy. He can enter, while he reads, into each author's point of view without either accepting or rejecting it, suspending when necessary his disbelief and (what is harder) his belief. But others lack this power. I must postpone a fuller consideration of their error till the next chapter.

Finally, what shall we say about the stigma of 'escapism'?

Now there is a clear sense in which all reading whatever is an escape. It involves a temporary transference of the mind from our actual surroundings to things merely imagined or conceived. This happens when we read history or science no less than when we read fictions. All such escape is *from* the same thing; immediate, concrete actuality. The important question is what we escape *to*. Some escape into egoistic castle-building. And this itself may be either harmless, if not very profitable, refreshment, or brutal, prurient and megalomaniac. Others escape into mere play, *divertissements* which may be exquisite works of art—the *Midsummer Night's Dream* or the *Nun's Priest's Tale*. Others, again, into what I call disinterested castle-building, 'conducted', by, say, the *Arcadia*, *The Shepheards Sirena*, or *The Ancient Mariner*. And others escape into realistic fictions. For, as Crabbe pointed out in a passage[1] not often enough quoted, a grim and distressful tale may offer a complete escape from the reader's actual distresses. Even a fiction that rivets our attention on 'life' or 'the present crisis' or 'the Age' may do this. For these, after all, are constructs, *entia rationis*; not facts on a level with the here and now, with my disquieting abdominal pain, the draught in this room, the pile of examination papers I have to mark, the bill I can't pay, the letter I don't know how to answer, and my bereaved or unrequited love. While I think of 'the Age', I forget these.

Escape, then, is common to many good and bad kinds of reading. By adding *-ism* to it, we suggest, I suppose, a confirmed habit of escaping too often, or for too long, or into the wrong things, or using escape as a substitute for action where action is appropriate, and thus neglecting real opportunities and evading real obligations. If so, we must judge each case on its merits. Escape is not necessarily joined to escapism. The authors who lead us

[1] *Tales*, Preface, para. 16.

furthest into impossible regions—Sidney, Spenser, and Morris—were men active and stirring in the real world. The Renaissance and our own nineteenth century, periods prolific in literary fantasy, were periods of great energy.

Since the charge of escapism against a very unrealistic work is sometimes varied or reinforced with that of childishness or (as they now say) 'infantilism', a word on that ambiguous accusation will not be amiss. Two points need to be made.

First, the association between fantasy (including *Märchen*) and childhood, the belief that children are the proper readers for this sort of work or that it is the proper reading for children, is modern and local. Most of the great fantasies and fairy-tales were not addressed to children at all, but to everyone. Professor Tolkien has described the real state of the case.[1] Certain kinds of furniture gravitated to the nursery when they became unfashionable among the adults; the fairy-tale has done the same. To imagine any special affinity between childhood and stories of the marvellous is like imagining a special affinity between childhood and Victorian sofas. If few but children now read such stories, that is not because children, as such, have a special predilection for them, but because children are indifferent to literary fashions. What we see in them is not a specifically childish taste, but simply a normal and perennial human taste, temporarily

[1] 'On Fairy-Stories', *Essays presented to Charles Williams* (1947), p. 58.

atrophied in their elders by a fashion. It is we, not they, whose taste needs explanation. And even to say this is to say too much. We ought, in strict truth, to say that some children, as well as some adults, like this genre, and that many children, like many adults, do not. For we must not be deceived by the contemporary practice of sorting books out according to the 'age-groups' for which they are supposed to be appropriate. That work is done by people who are not very curious about the real nature of literature nor very well acquainted with its history. It is a rough rule of thumb for the convenience of school-teachers, librarians, and the publicity departments in publishers' offices. Even as such it is very fallible. Instances that contradict it (in both directions) occur daily.

Secondly, if we are to use the words *childish* or *infantile* as terms of disapproval, we must make sure that they refer only to those characteristics of childhood which we become better and happier by outgrowing; not to those which every sane man would keep if he could and which some are fortunate for keeping. On the bodily level this is sufficiently obvious. We are glad to have outgrown the muscular weakness of childhood; but we envy those who retain its energy, its well-thatched scalp, its easily won sleeps, and its power of rapid recuperation. But surely the same is true on another level? The sooner we cease to be as fickle, as boastful, as jealous, as cruel, as ignorant, and as easily frightened as most children are, the better for us and for our neighbours. But who in his senses would not keep, if he could, that tireless curiosity, that intensity of imagination, that facility of suspending disbelief, that unspoiled appetite, that readiness to wonder, to pity, and to admire? The process of growing up is to be valued for what we gain, not for what we lose. Not to acquire a taste for the realistic is childish in the bad sense; to have lost the taste for marvels and adventures is no more a matter for congratulation than losing our teeth, our hair, our palate, and finally, our hopes. Why do we hear so much about the defects of immaturity and so little about those of senility?

When we accuse a work of infantilism we must, therefore, be careful what we mean. If we mean only that the taste for which it caters is one that usually appears early in life, that is nothing against the book. A taste is childish in the bad sense not because it develops at an early age but because, having some intrinsic defect in it, it ought to disappear as soon as possible. We call such a taste 'childish' because only childhood can excuse it, not because childhood can often achieve it. Indifference to dirt and untidiness is 'childish' because it is unhealthy and inconvenient and therefore ought to be speedily outgrown; a taste for bread and honey, though equally common in our salad days, is not. A taste for the comics is excusable only by extreme youth because it involves an acquiescence in hideous draughtsmanship and a scarcely human coarseness and flatness of narration. If you are going to call a taste for the marvellous childish in the same sense, you must similarly show its intrinsic badness. The dates at which our various traits develop are not a gauge of their value.

If they were, a very amusing result would follow. Nothing is more characteristically juvenile than contempt for juvenility. The eight-year-old despises the six-year-old and rejoices to be getting such a big boy; the schoolboy is very determined not to be a child, and the freshman not to be a schoolboy. If we are resolved to eradicate, without examining them on their merits, all the traits of our youth, we might begin with this—with youth's characteristic chronological snobbery. And what then would become of the criticism which attaches so much importance to being adult and instils a fear and shame of any enjoyment we can share with the very young?

VIII

ON MISREADING BY
THE LITERARY

WE must now return to the point which
I postponed in the last chapter. We have
to consider a fault in reading which cuts
right across our distinction between the literary and
the unliterary. Some of the former are guilty of it
and some of the latter are not.

Essentially, it involves a confusion between life
and art, even a failure to allow for the existence of
art at all. Its crudest form is pilloried in the old
story of the backwoodsman in the gallery who shot
the 'villain' on the stage. We see it also in the lowest
type of reader who wants sensational narrative but
will not accept it unless it is offered him as 'news'.
On a higher level it appears as the belief that all
good books are good primarily because they give
us knowledge, teach us 'truths' about 'life .
Dramatists and novelists are praised as if they were
doing, essentially, what used to be expected of
theologians and philosophers, and the qualities
which belong to their works as inventions and
as designs are neglected. They are reverenced as
teachers and insufficiently appreciated as artists.
In a word, De Quincey's 'literature of power'

74

is treated as a species within his 'literature of knowledge'.

We may begin by ruling out of consideration one way of treating fictions as sources of knowledge which, though not strictly literary, is pardonable at a certain age and usually transient. Between the ages of twelve and twenty nearly all of us acquired from novels, along with plenty of misinformation, a great deal of information about the world we live in: about the food, clothes, customs and climates of various countries, the working of various professions, about methods of travel, manners, law, and political machinery. We were getting not a philosophy of life but what is called 'general knowledge'. In a particular case a fiction may serve this purpose for even an adult reader. An inhabitant of the cruel countries might come to grasp our principle that a man is innocent till he is proved guilty from reading our detective stories (in that sense such stories are a great proof of real civilisation). But in general this use of fiction is abandoned as we grow older. The curiosities it used to satisfy have been satisfied or simply died away, or, if they survive, would now seek information from more reliable sources. That is one reason why we have less inclination to take up a new novel than we had in our youth.

Having got this special case out of the way, we may now return to the real subject.

It is obvious that some of the unliterary mistake

art for an account of real life. As we have seen, those whose reading is conducted, egoistic castle-building will inevitably do so. They wish to be deceived; they want to feel that though these beautiful things have not really happened to them, yet they might. ('He might take a fancy to me like that Duke did to that factory girl in the story.') But it is equally obvious that a great many of the un-literary are not in this state at all—are indeed almost safer from it than anyone else. Try the experiment on your grocer or gardener.You cannot often try it about a book, for he has read few, but a film will do just as well for our purpose. If you complain to him about the gross improbability of its happy ending, he will very probably reply 'Ah. I reckon they just put that in to wind it up like.' If you complain about the dull and perfunctory love-interest which has been thrust into a story of masculine adventure, he will say 'Oh well, you know, they usually got to put in a bit of that. The women like it.' He knows perfectly well that the film is art, not know-ledge. In a sense his very unliterariness saves him from confusing the two. He never expected the film to be anything but transitory, and not very important, entertainment; he never dreamed that any art could provide more than this. He goes to the pictures not to learn but to relax. The idea that any of his opinions about the real world could be modified by what he saw there would seem to him preposterous. Do you take him for a fool? Turn the conversation from art to life—gossip with him, bargain with him—and you will find he is as shrewd and realistic as you can wish.

Contrariwise, we find the error, in a subtle and especially insidious form, among the literary. When my pupils have talked to me about Tragedy (they have talked much less often, uncompelled, about tragedies), I have sometimes discovered a belief that it is valuable, is worth witnessing or reading, chiefly because it communicates something called the tragic 'view' or 'sense' or 'philosophy' of 'life'. This content is variously described, but in the most widely diffused version it seems to consist of two propositions: (1) That great miseries result from a flaw in the principal sufferer. (2) That these miseries, pushed to the extreme, reveal to us a certain splendour in man, or even in the universe. Though the anguish is great, it is at least not sordid, meaningless, or merely depressing.

No one denies that miseries with such a cause and such a close can occur in real life. But if tragedy is taken as a comment on life in the sense that we are meant to conclude from it 'This is the typical or usual, or ultimate, form of human misery', then tragedy becomes wishful moonshine. Flaws in character do cause suffering; but bombs and bayonets, cancer and polio, dictators and road-hogs, fluctuations in the value of money or in employment, and mere meaningless coincidence, cause a great deal more. Tribulation falls on the integrated

77

and well adjusted and prudent as readily as on anyone else. Nor do real miseries often end with a
curtain and a roll of drums 'in calm of mind, all
passion spent'. The dying seldom make magnificent
last speeches. And we who watch them die do not,
I think, behave very like the minor characters in a
tragic death-scene. For unfortunately the play is
not over. We have no *exeunt omnes*. The real story
does not end: it proceeds to ringing up under-
takers, paying bills, getting death certificates,
finding and proving a will, answering letters of
condolence. There is no grandeur and no finality.
Real sorrow ends neither with a bang nor a whim-
per. Sometimes, after a spiritual journey like Dante's,
down to the centre and then, terrace by terrace, up
the mountain of accepted pain, it may rise into
peace—but a peace hardly less severe than itself.
Sometimes it remains for life, a puddle in the mind
which grows always wider, shallower, and more
unwholesome. Sometimes it just peters out, as
other moods do. One of these alternatives has
grandeur, but not tragic grandeur. The other two—
ugly, slow, bathetic, unimpressive—would be of no
use at all to a dramatist. The tragedian dare not
present the totality of suffering as it usually is in its
uncouth mixture of agony with littleness, all the
indignities and (save for pity) the uninterestingness,
of grief. It would ruin his play. It would be merely
dull and depressing. He selects from the reality
just what his art needs; and what it needs is the

exceptional. Conversely, to approach anyone in real sorrow with these ideas about tragic grandeur, to insinuate that he is now assuming that 'sceptred pall', would be worse than imbecile: it would be odious.

Next to a world in which there were no sorrows we should like one where sorrows were always significant and sublime. But if we allow the 'tragic view of life' to make us believe that we live in such a world, we shall be deceived. Our very eyes teach us better. Where in all nature is there anything uglier and more undignified than an adult male face blubbered and distorted with weeping? And what's behind it is not much prettier. There is no sceptre and no pall.

It seems to me undeniable, that tragedy, taken as a philosophy of life, is the most obstinate and best camouflaged of all wish-fulfilments, just because its pretensions are so apparently realistic. The claim is that it has faced the worst. The conclusion that, despite the worst, some sublimity and significance remains, is therefore as convincing as the testimony of a witness who appears to speak against his will. But the claim that it has faced the worst—at any rate the commonest sort of 'worst'—is in my opinion simply false.

It is not the fault of the tragedians that this claim deceives certain readers, for the tragedians never made it. It is critics who make it. The tragedians chose for their themes stories (often grounded in the

79

mythical and impossible) suitable to the art they practised. Almost by definition, such stories would be atypical, striking, and in various other ways adapted to the purpose. Stories with a sublime and satisfying *finale* were chosen not because such a *finale* is characteristic of human misery, but because it is necessary to good drama.

It is probably from this view of tragedy that many young people derive the belief that tragedy is essentially 'truer to life' than comedy. This seems to me wholly unfounded. Each of these forms chooses out of real life just those sorts of events it needs. The raw materials are all around us, mixed anyhow. It is selection, isolation, and patterning, not a philosophy, that makes the two sorts of play. The two products do not contradict one another any more than two nosegays plucked out of the same garden. Contradiction comes in only when we (not the dramatists) turn them into propositions such as 'This is what human life is like'.

It may seem odd that the same people who think comedy less true than tragedy often regard broad farce as realistic. I have often met the opinion that in turning from the *Troilus* to his *faibliaux* Chaucer was drawing nearer to reality. I think this arises from a failure to distinguish between realism of presentation and realism of content. Chaucer's farce is rich in realism of presentation; not in that of content. Criseyde and Alisoun are equally probable women, but what happens in the *Troilus* is very much more probable than what happens in the *Miller's Tale*. The world of farce is hardly less ideal than that of pastoral. It is a paradise of jokes where the wildest coincidences are accepted and where all works together to produce laughter. Real life seldom succeeds in being, and never remains for more than a few minutes, nearly as funny as a well-invented farce. That is why the people feel that they cannot acknowledge the comicality of a real situation more emphatically than by saying 'It's as good as a play'.

All three forms of art make the abstractions proper to them. Tragedies omit the clumsy and apparently meaningless bludgeoning of much real misfortune and the prosaic littlenesses which usually rob real sorrows of their dignity. Comedies ignore the possibility that the marriage of lovers does not always lead to permanent, nor ever to perfect, happiness. Farce excludes pity for its butts in situations where, if they were real, they would deserve it. None of the three kinds is making a statement about life in general. They are all constructions: things made *out* of the stuff of real life; additions to life rather than comments on it.

At this point I must take pains not to be misunderstood. The great artist—or at all events the great literary artist—cannot be a man shallow either in his thoughts or his feelings. However improbable and abnormal a story he has chosen, it will, as we say, 'come to life' in his hands. The life to which it comes will be impregnated with all the wisdom, knowledge and experience the author has; and even more by something which I can only vaguely describe as the flavour or 'feel' that actual life has for him. It is this omnipresent flavour or feel that makes bad inventions so mawkish and suffocating, and good ones so tonic. The good ones allow us temporarily to share a sort of passionate sanity. And we may also—which is less important—expect to find in them many psychological truths and profound, at least profoundly felt, reflections. But all this comes to us, and was very possibly called out of the poet, as the 'spirit' (using that word in a quasi-chemical sense) of a work of art, a play. To formulate it as a philosophy, even if it were a rational philosophy, and regard the actual play as primarily a vehicle for that philosophy, is an outrage to the thing the poet has made for us.

I use the words *thing* and *made* advisedly. We have already mentioned, but not answered, the question whether a poem 'should not mean but be'. What guards the good reader from treating a tragedy—he will not talk much about an abstraction like 'Tragedy'—as a mere vehicle for truth is his continual awareness that it not only means, but is. It is not merely *logos* (something said) but *poiema* (something made). The same is true of a novel or narrative poem. They are complex and carefully made objects. Attention to the very objects they are is our first step. To value them chiefly for reflections which they may suggest to us or morals we may draw from them, is a flagrant instance of 'using' instead of 'receiving'.

What I mean by 'objects' need not remain mysterious. One of the prime achievements in every good fiction has nothing to do with truth or philosophy or a *Weltanschauung* at all. It is the triumphant adjustment of two different kinds of order. On the one hand, the events (the mere plot) have their chronological and causal order, that which they would have in real life. On the other, all the scenes or other divisions of the work must be related to each other according to principles of design, like the masses in a picture or the passages in a symphony. Our feelings and imaginations must be led through 'taste after taste, upheld with kindliest change'. Contrasts (but also premonitions and echoes) between the darker and the lighter, the swifter and the slower, the simpler and the more sophisticated, must have something like a balance, but never a too perfect symmetry, so that the shape of the whole work will be felt as inevitable and satisfying. Yet this second order must never confuse the first. The transition from the 'platform' to the court scene at the beginning of *Hamlet*, the placing of Aeneas' narrative in *Aeneid* II and III, or the darkness in the first two books of *Paradise Lost* leading to the ascent in the third, are simple illustrations. But there is yet another requisite. As little as possible must exist solely for the sake of other things. Every episode, explanation, description, dialogue—ideally every sentence—must be pleasure-able and interesting for its own sake. (A fault in Conrad's *Nostromo* is that we have to read so much pseudo-history before we get to the central matter, for which alone this history exists.)

Some will discount this as 'mere technique'. We must certainly agree that these orderings, apart from that which they order, are worse than 'mere'; they are nonentities, as shape is a nonentity apart from the body whose shape it is. But an 'appreciation' of sculpture which ignored the statue's shape in favour of the sculptor's 'view of life' would be self-deception. It is by the shape that it is a statue. Only because it is a statue do we come to be mentioning the sculptor's view of life at all.

It is very natural that when we have gone through the ordered movements which a great play or narrative excites in us—when we have danced that dance or enacted that ritual or submitted to that pattern—it should suggest to us many interesting reflections. We have 'put on mental muscle' as a result of this activity. We may thank Shakespeare or Dante for that muscle, but we had better not father on them the philosophical or ethical use we make of it. For one thing, this use is unlikely to rise very much—it may rise a little—above our own ordinary level. Many of the comments on life which people get out of Shakespeare could have been reached by very moderate talents without his assistance. For another, it may well impede future receptions of the work itself. We may go back to it chiefly to find further confirmation for our belief that it teaches this or that, rather than for a fresh immersion in what it is. We shall be like a man poking his fire, not to boil the kettle or warm the room, but in the hope of seeing in it the same pictures he saw yesterday. And since a text is 'but a cheverel glove' to a determined critic—since everything can be a symbol, or an irony, or an ambiguity—we shall easily find what we want. The supreme objection to this is that which lies against the popular use of all the arts. We are so busy doing things with the work that we give it too little chance to work on us. Thus increasingly we meet only ourselves.

But one of the chief operations of art is to remove our gaze from that mirrored face, to deliver us from that solitude. When we read the 'literature of knowledge' we hope, as a result, to think more correctly and clearly. In reading imaginative work, I suggest, we should be much less concerned with altering our own opinions—though this of course is sometimes their effect—than with entering fully into the opinions, and therefore also the attitudes, feelings and total experience, of other men. Who in his ordinary senses would try to decide between the claims of materialism and theism by reading Lucretius and Dante? But who in his literary senses would not delightedly learn from them a great deal about what it is like to be a materialist or a theist?

In good reading there ought to be no 'problem of belief'. I read Lucretius and Dante at a time when (by and large) I agreed with Lucretius. I have read them since I came (by and large) to agree with Dante. I cannot find that this has much altered my experience, or at all altered my evaluation, of either. A true lover of literature should be in one way like an honest examiner, who is prepared to give the highest marks to the telling, felicitous and well-documented exposition of views he dissents from or even abominates.

The sort of misreading I here protest against is unfortunately encouraged by the increasing importance of 'English Literature' as an academic discipline. This directs to the study of literature a great many talented, ingenious, and diligent people whose real interests are not specifically literary at all. Forced to talk incessantly about books, what can they do but try to make books into the sort of things they can talk about? Hence literature becomes for them a religion, a philosophy, a school of ethics, a psychotherapy, a sociology—anything rather than a collection of works of art. Lighter works—*divertissements*—are either disparaged or misrepresented as being really far more serious than they look. But to a real lover of literature an exquisitely made *divertissement* is a very much more respectable thing than some of the 'philosophies of life' which are foisted upon the great poets. For one thing, it is a good deal harder to make.

This is not to say that all critics who extract such a philosophy from their favourite novelists or poets produce work without value: Each attributes to his chosen author what he believes to be wisdom; and the sort of thing that seems to him wise will of course be determined by his own calibre. If he is a fool he will find and admire foolishness, if he is a mediocrity, platitude, in all his favourites. But if he is a profound thinker himself, what he acclaims and expounds as his author's philosophy may be well worth reading, even if it is in reality his own. We may compare him to the long succession of divines who have based edifying and eloquent sermons on some straining of their texts. The sermon, though bad exegesis, was often good homiletics in its own right.

IX

SURVEY

IT will now be convenient to sum up the position
I am trying to develop as follows:

1. A work of (whatever) art can be either
'received' or 'used'. When we 'receive' it we exert
our senses and imagination and various other powers
according to a pattern invented by the artist. When
we 'use' it we treat it as assistance for our own
activities. The one, to use an old-fashioned image,
is like being taken for a bicycle ride by a man who
may know roads we have never yet explored. The
other is like adding one of those little motor attach-
ments to our own bicycle and then going for one of
our familiar rides. These rides may in themselves be
good, bad, or indifferent. The 'uses' which the
many make of the arts may or may not be intrinsically vulgar, depraved, or morbid. That's as
may be. 'Using' is inferior to 'reception' because
art, if used rather than received, merely facilitates,
brightens, relieves or palliates our life, and does not
add to it.

2. When the art in question is literature a com-
plication arises, for to 'receive' significant words is
always, in one sense, to 'use' them, to go through
and beyond them to an imagined something which

is not itself verbal. The distinction here takes a somewhat different form. Let us call this 'imagined something' the *content*. The 'user' wants to use this content—as pastime for a dull or torturing hour, as a puzzle, as a help to castle-building, or perhaps as a source for 'philosophies of life'. The 'recipient' wants to rest in it. It is for him, at least temporarily, an end. That way, it may be compared (upward) with religious contemplation or (downward) with a game.

3. But, paradoxically, the 'user' never makes a full use of the words and indeed prefers words of which no really full use could be made. A very rough and ready apprehension of the content is enough for his purpose because he wants only to use it for his present need. Whatever in the words invites a more precise apprehension, he ignores; whatever demands it, is a stumbling-block. Words are to him mere pointers or signposts. In the good reading of a good book, on the other hand, though they certainly point, words do something for which 'pointing' is far too coarse a name. They are exquisitely detailed compulsions on a mind willing and able to be so compelled. That is why to speak of 'magic' or 'evocation' in connection with a style is to use a metaphor not merely emotive, but extremely apt. That is why, again, we are driven to speak of the 'colour', 'flavour', 'texture', 'smell' or 'race' of words. That is why the inevitable abstraction of content and words seems to do such violence to great

literature. Words, we want to protest, are more than the clothing, more even than the incarnation, of content. And this is true. As well try to separate the shape and colour of an orange. Yet for some purposes we must separate them in thought.

4. Because good words can thus compel, thus guide us into every cranny of a character's mind or make palpable and individual Dante's Hell or Pindar's gods'-eye view of an island,[1] good reading is always aural as well as visual. For the sound is not merely a superadded pleasure, though it may be that too, but part of the compulsion; in that sense, part of the meaning. This is true even of a good, working prose. What keeps us happy, despite much shallowness and bluster, through a Shavian preface, is the brisk, engaging and cheerful cocksureness; and this reaches us mainly through the rhythm. What makes Gibbon so exhilarating is the sense of triumph, of ordering and contemplating in Olympian tranquillity so many miseries and grandeurs. It is the periods that do it. Each is like a great viaduct on which we pass, smoothly and at unaltered speed, over smiling or appalling valleys.

5. What bad reading wholly consists in may enter as an ingredient into good reading. Excitement and curiosity obviously do. So does vicarious happiness; not that good readers ever read for the sake of it, but that when happiness legitimately occurs in a fiction they enter into it. But when they demand a happy

[1] *Fragm.* 87 + 88 (58).

ending it will not be for this reason but because it seems to them in various ways demanded by the work itself. (Deaths and disasters can be as patently 'contrived' and inharmonious as wedding bells.) Egoistic castle-building will not survive long in the right reader. But I suspect that, especially in youth, or other unhappy periods, it may send him to a book. It has been maintained that the attraction of Trollope or even Jane Austen for many readers is the imaginative truancy into an age when their class, or the class they identify with theirs, was more secure and fortunate than now. Perhaps it is sometimes so with Henry James. In some of his books the protagonists live a life as impossible for most of us as that of fairies or butterflies; free from religion, from work, from economic cares, from the demands of family and settled neighbourhood. But it can only be an initial attraction. No one who chiefly or even very strongly wants egoistic castle-building will persevere long with James, Jane Austen, or Trollope.

In characterising the two sorts of reading I have deliberately avoided the word 'entertainment'. Even when fortified by the adjective *mere*, it is too equivocal. If entertainment means light and playful pleasure, then I think it is exactly what we ought to get from some literary work—say, from a trifle by Prior or Martial. If it means those things which 'grip' the reader of popular romance—suspense, excitement and so forth—then I would say that every book should be entertaining. A good book will be more; it must not be less. Entertainment, in this sense, is like a qualifying examination. If a fiction can't provide even that, we may be excused from inquiry into its higher qualities. But of course what 'grips' one will not grip another. Where the intelligent reader holds his breath, the duller one may complain that nothing is happening. But I hope that most of what is usually called (in disparagement) 'entertainment' will find a place among my classifications.

I have also refrained from describing the sort of reading I approve as 'critical reading'. The phrase, if not elliptically used, seems to me deeply misleading. I said in an earlier chapter that we can judge any sentence or even word only by the work it does or fails to do. The effect must precede the judgement on the effect. The same is true of a whole work. Ideally, we must receive it first and then evaluate it. Otherwise, we have nothing to evaluate. Unfortunately this ideal is progressively less and less realised the longer we live in a literary profession or in literary circles. It occurs, magnificently, in young readers. At a first reading of some great work, they are 'knocked flat'. Criticise it? No, by God, but read it again. The judgement 'This must be a great work' may be long delayed. But in later life we can hardly help evaluating as we go along; it has become a habit. We thus fail of that inner silence, that emptying out of ourselves, by which we ought to make room for the total reception of the work. The failure is greatly aggravated if, while we read, we know that we are under some obligation to express a judgement; as when we read a book in order to review it, or a friend's MS. in order to advise him. Then the pencil gets to work on the margin and phrases of censure or approval begin forming themselves in our mind. All this activity impedes reception.

For this reason I am very doubtful whether criticism is a proper exercise for boys and girls. A clever schoolboy's reaction to his reading is most naturally expressed by parody or imitation. The necessary condition of all good reading is 'to get ourselves out of the way'; we do not help the young to do this by forcing them to keep on expressing opinions. Especially poisonous is the kind of teaching which encourages them to approach every literary work with suspicion. It springs from a very reasonable motive. In a world full of sophistry and propaganda, we want to protect the rising genera-tion from being deceived, to forearm them against the invitations to false sentiment and muddled thinking which printed words will so often offer them. Unfortunately, the very same habit which makes them impervious to the bad writing may make them impervious also to the good. The exces-sively 'knowing' rustic who comes to town too well primed with warnings against coney-catchers does not always get on very well; indeed, after reject-ing much genuine friendliness, missing many real opportunities and making several enemies, he is quite likely to fall a victim to some trickster who flatters his 'shrewdness'. So here. No poem will give up its secret to a reader who enters it regarding the poet as a potential deceiver, and determined not to be taken in. We must risk being taken in, if we are to get anything. The best safeguard against bad literature is a full experience of good; just as a real and affectionate acquaintance with honest people gives a better protection against rogues than a habitual distrust of everyone.

To be sure, boys do not reveal the disabling effect of such a training by condemning all the poems their masters set before them. A mixture of images which resists logic and visual imagination will be praised if they meet it in Shakespeare and triumphantly 'exposed' if they meet it in Shelley. But that is because the boys know what is expected of them. They know, on quite other grounds, that Shakespeare has to be praised and Shelley condemned. They get the right answer not because their method leads to it, but because they knew it beforehand. Sometimes, when they don't, a revealing answer may give the teacher cold doubts about the method itself.

X

POETRY

BUT have I not made a startling omission? Poets and poems have been mentioned, but I have not said a word about poetry as such.

Notice, however, that nearly all the questions we have discussed would have been regarded by Aristotle, Horace, Tasso, Sidney and perhaps Boileau, as questions which, if they were to be raised at all, would properly come in a treatise 'On Poetry'.

Remember, too, that we have been concerned with literary and unliterary modes of reading. And unhappily this topic can be almost fully treated without mentioning poetry, for the unliterary hardly read it at all. A few here and there, all women and mostly old women, may embarrass us by repeating the verses of Ella Wheeler Wilcox or Patience Strong. The poetry they like is always gnomic and thus, very literally, a comment on life. They use it rather as their grandmothers would have used proverbs or biblical texts. Their feelings are not much engaged; their imagination, I believe, not at all. This is the little trickle or puddle still left in the dry bed where ballad and nursery-rhyme and pro-verbial jingle once flowed. But it is now so tiny that it hardly deserves mention in a book on this scale. In general the unliterary do not read poetry. A growing number of those who are in other respects literary do not read poetry. And modern poetry is read by very few who are not themselves poets, professional critics, or teachers of literature.

These facts have a common significance. The arts, as they develop, grow further apart. Once, song, poetry, and dance were all parts of a single *dromenon*. Each has become what it now is by separation from the others, and this has involved great losses and great gains. Within the single art of literature, the same process has taken place. Poetry has differentiated itself more and more from prose.

This sounds paradoxical if we are thinking chiefly of diction. Ever since Wordsworth's time the special vocabulary and syntax which poets once were allowed to use have been subjected to attack, and they are now completely banished. In that way poetry may be said to be nearer to prose than ever before. But the approximation is superficial and the next gust of fashion may blow it away. Though the modern poet does not, like Pope, use *e'er* and *oft* nor call a young woman a *nymph*, his productions have really far less in common with any prose work than Pope's poetry had. The story of *The Rape of the Lock*, sylphs and all, could have been told, though not so effectively, in prose. The *Odyssey* and the *Comedy* have something to say that could have been said well, though not equally well, without verse. Most of the qualities Aristotle demands of a tragedy could occur in a prose play. Poetry and prose, however different in language, overlapped, almost coincided, in content. But modern poetry, if it 'says' anything at all, if it aspires to 'mean' as well as to 'be', says what prose could not say in any fashion. To read the old poetry involved learning a slightly different language; to read the new involves the unmaking of your mind, the abandonment of all the logical and narrative connections which you use in reading prose or in conversation. You must achieve a trance-like condition in which images, associations, and sounds operate without these. Thus the common ground between poetry and any other use of words is reduced almost to zero. In that way poetry is now more quintessentially poetical than ever before; 'purer' in the negative sense. It not only does (like all good poetry) what prose can't do: it deliberately refrains from doing anything that prose can do.

Unfortunately, but inevitably, this process is accompanied by a steady diminution in the number of its readers. Some have blamed the poets for this, and some the people. I am not sure that there need be any question of blame. The more any instrument is refined and perfected for some particular function, the fewer those who have the skill, or the occasion, to handle it must of course become. Many use ordinary knives and few use surgeons' scalpels.

The scalpel is better for operations, but it is no good for anything else. Poetry confines itself more and more to what only poetry can do; but this turns out to be something which not many people want done. Nor, of course, could they receive it if they did. Modern poetry is too difficult for them. It is idle to complain; poetry so pure as this must be difficult. But neither must the poets complain if they are unread. When the art of reading poetry requires talents hardly less exalted than the art of writing it, readers cannot be much more numerous than poets. If you write a piece for the fiddle that only one performer in a hundred can play you must not expect to hear it very often performed. The musical analogy is no longer a remote one. Modern poetry is such that the *cognoscenti* who explicate it can read the same piece in utterly different ways. We can no longer assume all but one of these readings, or else all, to be 'wrong'. The poem, clearly, is like a score and the readings like performances. Different renderings are admissible. The question is not which is the 'right' one but which is the best. The explicators are more like conductors of an orchestra than members of an audience.

The hope that this state of affairs may be transient dies hard. Some, who dislike modern poetry, hope that it will soon perish, asphyxiated in the vacuum of its own purity, and give place to a poetry which will overlap more largely with the passions and interests of which the laity are conscious. Others, that by 'culture' the laity may be 'raised' till poetry, as it now is, can again have a reasonably wide public. I myself am haunted by a third possibility.

The ancient city states developed, under the spur of practical necessity, great skill in speaking so as to be audible and persuasive to large assemblies in the open air. They called it Rhetoric. Rhetoric became part of their education. After a few centuries conditions changed and the uses of this art disappeared. But its status, as part of the educational curriculum, remained. It remained for more than a thousand years. It is not impossible that poetry, as the moderns practise it, may have a similar destiny before it. The explication of poetry is already well entrenched as a scholastic and academic exercise. The intention to keep it there, to make proficiency in it the indispensable qualification for white-collared jobs, and thus to secure for poets and their explicators a large and permanent (because a conscript) audience, is avowed.[1] It may possibly succeed. Without coming home any more than it now does to the 'business and bosoms' of most men, poetry may, in this fashion, reign for a millennium; providing material for the explication which teachers will praise as an incomparable discipline and pupils will accept as a necessary *moyen de parvenir*.

But this is speculation. For the moment, poetry's area in the map of reading has shrunk from that of

[1] See J. W. Saunders, 'Poetry in the Managerial Age', *Essays in Criticism*, IV, 3 (July 1954).

a great empire to that of a tiny province—a province which, as it grows smaller, emphasises its difference from all other places more and more, till in the end this combination of exiguous size and local peculiarity suggests not so much a province as a 'reservation'. Not *simpliciter*, but for the purpose of certain broad geographical generalisations, such a region is negligible. Within it we cannot study the difference between unliterary and literary readers, for there are no unliterary readers there.

Nevertheless, we have already seen that the literary sometimes fall into what I think bad modes of reading, and even that these are sometimes subtler forms of the same errors that the unliterary commit. They may do so when reading poems.

The literary sometimes 'use' poetry instead of 'receiving' it. They differ from the unliterary because they know very well what they are doing and are prepared to defend it. 'Why', they ask, 'should I turn from a real and present experience— what the poem means to me, what happens to me when I read it—to inquiries about the poet's intention or reconstructions, always uncertain, of what it may have meant to his contemporaries?' There seem to be two answers. One is that the poem in my head which I make from my mistranslations of Chaucer or misunderstandings of Donne may possibly not be so good as the work Chaucer or Donne actually made. Secondly, why not have both? After enjoying what I made of it, why not go back to the text, this time looking up the hard words, puzzling out the allusions, and discovering that some metrical delights in my first experience were due to my fortunate mispronunciations, and see whether I can enjoy the poet's poem, not necessarily instead of, but in addition to, my own one? If I am a man of genius and uninhibited by false modesty I may still think my poem the better of the two. But I could not have discovered this without knowing both. Often, both are well worth retaining. Do we not all still enjoy certain effects which passages in classical or foreign poets produced in us when we misunderstood them? We know better now. We enjoy something, we trust, more like what Virgil or Ronsard meant to give us. This does not abolish or stain the old beauty. It is rather like revisiting a beautiful place we knew in childhood. We appraise the landscape with an adult eye; we also revive the pleasures—often very different—which it produced when we were small children.

Admittedly, we can never quite get out of our own skins. Whatever we do, something of our own and of our age's making will remain in our experience of all literature. Equally, I can never see anything exactly from the point of view even of those whom I know and love best. But I can make at least some progress towards it. I can eliminate at least the grosser illusions of perspective. Literature helps me to do it with live people, and live people help me to do it with literature. If I can't get out of the dungeon I shall at least look out through the bars. It is better than sinking back on the straw in the darkest corner.

There may, however, be poems (modern poems) which actually demand the sort of reading I have condemned. The words, perhaps, were never meant as anything but raw material for whatever each reader's sensibility may make of them, and there was no intention that one reader's experience should have anything in common with another's or with the poet's. If so, then no doubt this sort of reading would be proper for them. It is a pity if a glazed picture is so placed that you see in it only your own reflection; it is not a pity when a mirror is so placed.

We found fault with the unliterary for reading with insufficient attention to the actual words. This fault, as a whole, never occurs when the literary are reading poetry. They attend very fully to the words in various ways. But I have sometimes found that their aural character is not fully received. I do not think it is neglected through inattention; rather, it is deliberately ignored. I have heard a member of the English Faculty in a university say openly 'Whatever else matters in poetry, the sound doesn't'. Perhaps that was only his fun. But I have also found as an examiner that a surprising number of Honours candidates, certainly in other respects literary people, betray by their misquotations a total unconsciousness of metre.

How has this astonishing state of affairs come

about? I offer a guess at two possible causes. At some schools children are taught to write out poetry they have learned for repetition not according to the lines but in 'speech-groups'. The purpose is to cure them of what is called 'sing-song'. This seems a very short-sighted policy. If these children are going to be lovers of poetry when they grow up, sing-song will cure itself in due time, and if they are not it doesn't matter. In childhood sing-song is not a defect. It is simply the first form of rhythmical sensibility; crude itself, but a good symptom not a bad one. This metronomic regularity, this sway of the whole body to the metre simply as metre, is the basis which makes possible all later variations and subtleties. For there are no variations except for those who know a norm, and no subtleties for those who have not grasped the obvious. Again, it is possible that those who are now young have met *vers libre* too early in life. When this is real poetry, its aural effects are of extreme delicacy and demand for their appreciation an ear long trained on metrical poetry. Those who think they can receive *vers libre* without a metrical training are, I submit, deceiving themselves; trying to run before they can walk. But in literal running the falls hurt, and the would-be runner discovers his mistake. It is not so with a reader's self-deceptions. While he falls he can still believe himself to be running. As a result he may never learn to walk, and therefore never learn to run, at all.

XI

THE EXPERIMENT

THE apparatus which my experiment required has now been assembled and we can get to work. Normally we judge men's literary taste by the things they read. The question was whether there might be some advantage in reversing the process and judging literature by the way men read it. If all went ideally well we should end by defining good literature as that which permits, invites, or even compels good reading; and bad, as that which does the same for bad reading. This is an ideal simplification, and we shall have to be content with something less neat. For the moment, however, I want to submit the possible utility of this reversal.

First, it fixes our attention on the act of reading. Whatever the value of literature may be, it is actual only when and where good readers read. Books on a shelf are only potential literature. Literary taste is only a potentiality when we are not reading. Neither potentiality is called into act except in this transient experience. If literary scholarship and criticism are regarded as activities ancillary to literature, then their sole function is to multiply, prolong, and safeguard experiences of good reading. A system which heads us off from abstraction by being centred on literature in operation is what we need.

Secondly, the proposed system puts our feet on solid ground, whereas the usual one puts them on a quicksand. You discover that I like Lamb. Being sure that Lamb is bad, you say my taste is bad. But your view of Lamb is either an isolated personal reaction, just like my view of him, or else based on the prevalent view of the literary world. If the former, your condemnation of my taste is insolent; only manners deter me from a *tu quoque*. But if you take your stand on the 'prevalent' view, how long do you suppose it will prevail? You know that Lamb would not have been a black mark against me fifty years ago. You know that Tennyson would have been a far blacker mark in the thirties than he is now: that dethronements and restorations are almost monthly events. You can trust none of them to be permanent. Pope came in, went out, came back. Milton, hanged, drawn and quartered by two or three influential critics—and their disciples all said Amen—seems to have revived. Kipling's stock, once very high, fell to the bottom of the market, and now there are signs of a faint rise. 'Taste' in this sense is mainly a chronological phenomenon. Tell me the date of your birth and I can make a shrewd guess whether you prefer Hopkins or Housman, Hardy or Lawrence. Tell me that a man despised Pope and admired Ossian, and I shall make a good shot at his *floruit*. All you can really say about my taste is that it is old fashioned; yours will soon be the same.

But suppose you had gone quite a different way to work. Suppose you had given me enough rope and let me hang myself. You might have encouraged me to talk about Lamb, discovered that I was ignoring some things he really has and reading into him a good many that aren't there, that I seldom in fact read what I so praised, and that the very terms in which I praised it revealed how completely it was for me a mere stimulant to wistful-whimsical reveries of my own. And suppose that you then went round applying the same methods of detection to other admirers of Lamb, and each time got the same result. If you had done this, then, though you would never reach a mathematical certainty, you would have solid ground for a steadily growing conviction that Lamb is bad. You would argue 'Since all who enjoy Lamb do so by applying to him the worst kind of reading, Lamb is probably a bad author'. Observation of how men read is a strong basis for judgements on what they read; but judgements on what they read is a flimsy, even a momentary, basis for judgements on their way of reading. For the accepted valuation of literary works varies with every change of fashion, but the distinction between attentive and inattentive, obedient and wilful, disinterested and egoistic, modes of reading is permanent; if ever valid, valid everywhere and always.

Thirdly, it would make critical condemnation a laborious task, and this I reckon an advantage. It is now too easy.

Whichever method we use, whether we judge books by their readers or vice versa, we always make a double distinction. We first separate the sheep from the goats and then the better sheep from the worse. We put some readers or books beyond the pale, and then distribute praise and blame on those within it. Thus, if we start with books, we draw a line between mere 'commercial trash', thrillers, pornography, short stories in the women's magazines, etc., and what may be called 'polite' or 'adult' or 'real' or 'serious' literature. But then we call some of the latter good and some bad. The most approved modern criticism, for example, would call Morris and Housman bad, Hopkins and Rilke good. If we are judging readers we do the same. We make a broad, and hardly disputable, division between those who read seldom, hastily, hazily, forgetfully, only to kill time, and those to whom reading is an arduous and important activity. But then, within the latter class, we distinguish 'good' from 'bad' taste.

In making the first distinction, drawing the pale, a critic who works by the present system must claim that he is judging books. But in fact the books he puts beyond the pale are mostly books he has never read. How many 'westerns' have you read? How much science-fiction? If such a critic is guided simply by the low prices of these books and the lurid pictures on their jackets, he is on very insecure ground. He may chance to cut a poor figure in the eyes of posterity, for a work which was mere commercial trash to the *cognoscenti* of one generation might possibly become a classic to those of another. If, on the other hand, he is guided by a contempt for the readers of such books, then he is making a crude and unacknowledged use of my system. It would be safer to admit what he was doing and do it better; make sure that his contempt had in it no admixture of merely social snobbery or intellectual priggery. My proposed system works in the open. If we cannot observe the reading habits of those who buy the Westerns, or don't think it worth while to try, we say nothing about the books. If we can, there is usually not much difficulty in assigning those habits either to the unliterary or the literary class. If we find that a book is usually read in one way, still more if we never find that it is read in the other, we have a prima facie case for thinking it bad. If on the other hand we found even one reader to whom the cheap little book with its double columns and the lurid daub on its cover had been a lifelong delight, who had read and reread it, who would notice, and object, if a single word were changed, then, however little we could see in it ourselves and however it was despised by our friends and colleagues, we should not dare to put it beyond the pale.

How risky the current method can be, I have

some reason to know. Science-fiction is a literary province I used to visit fairly often; if I now visit it seldom, that is not because my taste has improved but because the province has changed, being now covered with new building estates, in a style I don't care for. But in the good old days I noticed that whenever critics said anything about it, they betrayed great ignorance. They talked as if it were a homogeneous genre. But it is not, in the literary sense, a genre at all. There is nothing common to all who write it except the use of a particular 'machine'. Some of the writers are of the family of Jules Verne and are primarily interested in technology. Some use the machine simply for literary fantasy and produce what is essentially *Märchen* or myth. A great many use it for satire; nearly all the most pungent American criticism of the American way of life takes this form, and would at once be denounced as un-American if it ventured into any other. And finally, there is the great mass of hacks who merely 'cashed in' on the boom in science-fiction and used remote planets or even galaxies as the backcloth for spy-stories or love-stories which might as well or better have been located in Whitechapel or the Bronx. And as the stories differ in kind, so of course do their readers. You can, if you wish, class all science-fiction together; but it is about as perceptive as classing the works of Ballantyne, Conrad and W. W. Jacobs together as 'the sea-story' and then criticising *that*.

But it is when we come to the second distinction, that made among the sheep or within the pale, that my system would differ most sharply from the established one. For the established system, the difference between distinctions within the pale and that primary distinction which draws the pale itself, can only be one of degree. Milton is bad and Patience Strong is worse; Dickens (most of him) is bad and Edgar Wallace is worse. My taste is bad because I like Scott and Stevenson; the taste of those who like E. R. Burroughs is worse. But the system I propose would draw a distinction not of degree but of kind between readings. All the words —'taste', 'liking', 'enjoyment'—bear different meanings as applied to the unliterary and to me. There is no evidence that anyone has ever reacted to Edgar Wallace as I react to Stevenson. In that way, the judgement that someone is unliterary is like the judgement 'This man is not in love', whereas the judgement that my taste is bad is more like 'This man is in love, but with a frightful woman'. And just as the mere fact that a man of sense and breeding loves a woman we dislike properly and inevitably makes us consider her again and look for, and sometimes find, something in her we had not noticed before, so, in my system, the very fact that people, or even any one person, can well and truly read, and love for a lifetime, a book we had thought bad, will raise the suspicion that it cannot really be as bad as we thought. Sometimes, to be sure, our friend's mistress remains in our eyes so plain, stupid and disagreeable that we can attribute his love only to the irrational and mysterious behaviour of hormones; similarly, the book he likes may continue to seem so bad that we have to attribute his liking to some early association or other psychological accident. But we must, and should, remain uncertain. Always, there may be something in it that we can't see. The prima facie probability that anything which has ever been truly read and obstinately loved by any reader has some virtue in it is overwhelming. To condemn such a book is therefore, on my system, a very serious matter. Our condemnation is never quite final. The question could always without absurdity be re-opened.

And here, I suggest, the proposed system is the more realistic. For, whatever we say, we are all aware in a cool hour that the distinctions within the pale are far more precarious than the location of the pale itself, and that nothing whatever is gained by disguising the fact. When whistling to keep our spirits up, we may say that we are as certain of Tennyson's inferiority to Wordsworth as of Edgar Wallace's to Balzac. When heated with controversy you may say that my taste in liking Milton is merely a milder instance of the same sort of badness we attribute to the taste that likes the comics. We can say these things but no sane man quite fully believes them. The distinctions we draw between better and worse within the pale are not at all like that between 'trash' and 'real' literature. They all depend on precarious and reversible judgements. The proposed system frankly acknowledges this. It admits from the outset that there can be no question of totally and finally 'debunking' or 'exposing' any author who has for some time been well inside the pale. We start from the assumption that whatever has been found good by those who really and truly read probably is good. All probability is against those who attack. And all they can hope to do is to persuade people that it is less good than they think; freely confessing that even this assessment may presently be set aside.

Thus one result of my system would be to silence the type of critic for whom all the great names in English literature—except for the half dozen protected by the momentary critical 'establishment'—are as so many lamp-posts for a dog. And this I consider a good thing. These dethronements are a great waste of energy. Their acrimony produces heat at the expense of light. They do not improve anyone's capacity for good reading. The real way of mending a man's taste is not to denigrate his present favourites but to teach him how to enjoy something better.

Such are the advantages I think we might hope from basing our criticism of books on our criticism of reading. But we have so far pictured the system working ideally and ignored the snags. In practice we shall have to be content with something less.

The most obvious objection to judging books by the way they are read is the fact that the same book may be read in different ways. We all know that certain passages in good fiction and good poetry are used by some readers, chiefly schoolboys, as pornography; and now that Lawrence is coming out in paperbacks, the pictures on their covers and the company they keep on the station bookstalls show very clearly what sort of sales, and therefore what sort of reading, the booksellers anticipate. We must, therefore, say that what damns a book is not the existence of bad readings but the absence of good ones. Ideally, we should like to define a good book as one which 'permits, invites, or compels' good reading. But we shall have to make do with 'permits and invites'. There may indeed be books which compel a good reading in the sense that no one who reads in the wrong way would be likely to get through more than a few of their pages. If you took up *Samson Agonistes*, *Rasselas*, or *Urn Burial* to pass the time, or for excitement, or as an aid to egoistic castle-building you would soon put it down. But books which thus resist bad reading are not necessarily better than books which do not. It is, logically, an accident that some beauties can, and others cannot, be abused. As for 'invites', invitation admits of degrees. 'Permits' is therefore our sheet-anchor. The ideally bad book is the one of which a good reading is impossible. The words in which it exists will not bear close attention, and what they communicate offers you nothing unless you are prepared either for mere thrills or for flattering daydreams. But 'invitation' comes into our conception of a good book. It is not enough that attentive and obedient reading should be barely possible if we try hard enough. The author must not leave us to do all the work. He must show, and pretty quickly, that his writing deserves, because it rewards, alert and disciplined reading.

It will also be objected that to take our stand upon readings rather than books is to turn from the known to the unknowable. The books, after all, are obtainable and we can inspect them for ourselves; what can we really know about other people's ways of reading? But this objection is not so formidable as it sounds.

The judgement of readings, as I have already said, is twofold. First, we put some readers outside the pale as unliterary; then we distinguish better and worse tastes within the pale. When we are doing the first, the readers themselves will give us no conscious assistance. They do not talk about reading and would be inarticulate if they tried to. But in their case external observation is perfectly easy. Where reading plays a very small part in the total life and every book is tossed aside like an old newspaper the moment it has been used, unliterary reading can be diagnosed with certainty. Where there is passionate and constant love of a book and rereading, then, however bad we think the book and however immature or uneducated we think the reader, it cannot. (By rereading I mean, of course, rereading for choice. A lonely child in a house where there are few books or a ship's officer on a long voyage may be driven to reread anything *faute de mieux*.)

When we are making the second distinction—approving or censuring the tastes of those who are obviously literary—the test by external observation fails us. But to compensate for that, we are now dealing with articulate people. They will talk, and even write, about their favourite books. They will sometimes explicitly tell us, and more often unintentionally reveal, the sort of pleasure they take in them and the sort of reading it implies. We can thus often judge, not with certainty but with great probability, who has received Lawrence on his literary merits and who is primarily attracted by the *imago* of Rebel or Poor Boy Makes Good; who loves Dante as a poet and who loves him as a Thomist; who seeks in an author the enlargement of his mental being and who seeks only the enlargement of his self-esteem. When all, or most, of a writer's eulogists betray unliterary, or anti-literary, or extra-literary motives for their *penchant*, we shall have just suspicions of the book.

Of course we shall not abstain from the experiment of reading it ourselves. But we shall do this in a particular way. Nothing is less illuminating than to read some author who is at present under a cloud (Shelley, say, or Chesterton) for the purpose of confirming the bad opinion we already had of him. The result is a foregone conclusion. If you already distrust the man you are going to meet, everything he says or does will seem to confirm your suspicions. We can find a book bad only by reading it as if it might, after all, be very good. We must empty our minds and lay ourselves open. There is no work in which holes can't be picked; no work that can succeed without a preliminary act of good will on the part of the reader.

You may ask whether we should take so much trouble with a work which is almost certainly bad on the bare hundredth chance that it may have some goodness in it. But there is no reason at all why we should, unless of course we are going to pass judgement on it. No one asks you to hear the evidence in every case that goes through the courts. But if you are on the bench, still more if you have volunteered for that position, I think you should. No one obliges me to assess Martin Tupper or Amanda Ross; but if I am going to, I must read them fairly.

Inevitably all this will seem to some an elaborate device for protecting bad books from the castigation they richly deserve. It may even be thought I have an eye to my own darlings or those of my friends. I can't help that. I want to convince people that adverse judgements are always the most hazardous, because I believe this is the truth. And it ought to be obvious why adverse judgements are so hazardous. A negative proposition is harder to establish than a positive. One glance may enable us to say there is a spider in the room; we should need a spring-cleaning (at least) before we could say with certainty that there wasn't. When we pronounce a book good we have a positive experience of our own to go upon. We have found ourselves enabled, and invited, and perhaps compelled to what we think thoroughly good reading; at any rate, to the best reading we are capable of. Though a modest doubt as to the quality even of our best may, and should, remain we can hardly be mistaken as to which of our readings are better and which worse. But in order to pronounce a book bad it is not enough to discover that it elicits no good response from ourselves, for that might be our fault. In calling the book bad we are claiming not that it can elicit bad reading, but that it can't elicit good. This negative proposition can never be certain. I may say 'If I were to take pleasure in this book it could be only the pleasure of transitory thrills, or wishful reverie, or agreement with the author's opinions'. But others may be able to do with it what I can't.

By an unfortunate paradox the most refined and sensitive criticism is as exposed as any other to this particular hazard. Such criticism (quite rightly) ponders every word and judges an author by his style in a sense very different from that of the Style-monger. It is on the look-out for all the implications or overtones by which a word or a phrase may betray faults of attitude in the author. Nothing, in itself, could be more just. But then the critic needs to be certain that the fine shades which he detects are really current beyond his own circle. The more refined the critic is, the more likely it is that he lives in a very small circle of *littérateurs* who constantly meet and read one another and who have developed what is almost a private language. If the author is not himself in the same set—and he could be a man of letters and a man of genius without knowing of its existence—his words will have all manner of overtones for such critics which simply did not exist for him or for anyone he ever talked to. I was lately accused of facetiousness for putting a phrase in inverted commas. I did so because I believed it to be an Americanism not yet Anglicised even for colloquial use. I used inverted commas just as I would have used italics for a scrap of French; italics I could not use, because readers might have thought they were meant for emphasis. If my critic had said this was clumsy he might have been right. But the charge of facetiousness revealed that he and I were at cross purposes. Where I come from no one has ever thought inverted commas funny; unnecessary, wrongly used perhaps, but not funny. My guess is that where my critic comes from they are invariably used to imply some sort of derision; and also, perhaps, that what to me was a bit of foreign language is to him perfectly current. And this sort of thing, I fancy, is not unusual. The critics assume that the use of English common in their own set—a use which is really very esoteric, not always very convenient, and always in rapid change—is common to all educated men. They find symptoms of the author's hidden attitudes where there are in reality only symptoms of his age or his remoteness from London. He fares among them like a stranger who quite innocently says something by which, in the college or the family where he is dining, there hangs a tale—a joke or a tragedy he could not possibly know. 'Reading between the lines' is inevitable, but we must practise it with great caution, or we may find mares' nests.

It is not to be denied that the system I propose, and the whole spirit of that system, must tend to moderate our belief in the utility of strictly evaluative criticism, and especially of its condemnations. Evaluative critics, though they alone have an etymological right to the name, are not the only people called critics. Evaluation plays a minor part in Arnold's conception of criticism. Criticism is for him 'essentially' the exercise of curiosity, which he defines as the 'disinterested love of a free play of the mind on all subjects for its own sake'.[1] The important thing is 'to see the object as in itself it really is'.[2] It matters more to see precisely what sort of poet Homer is than to tell the world how much it ought to like that sort of poet. The best value

[1] *Function of Criticism.*   [2] *On Translating Homer*, II.

judgement is that 'which almost insensibly forms itself in a fair and clear mind, along with fresh knowledge'.[1] If criticism in Arnold's sense has been adequate both in quantity and quality, criticism in the sense of evaluation will hardly be needed. Least of all is it the critic's function to press his evaluations upon others. 'The great art of criticism is to get oneself out of the way and to let humanity decide.'[2] We are to show others the work they claim to admire or despise as it really is; to describe, almost to define, its character, and then leave them to their own (now better informed) reactions. In one place the critic is even warned not to adopt a ruthless perfectionism. He 'is to keep his idea of the best, of perfection, and at the same time to be willingly accessible to every second best which offers itself'.[3] He is, in a word, to have the character which Mac-Donald attributed to God, and Chesterton, following him, to the critic; that of being 'easy to please, but hard to satisfy'.

Criticism as Arnold conceived it (whatever we may think of his own practice) I take to be a very useful activity. The question is about the criticism which pronounces on the merits of books; about evaluations, and devaluations. Such criticism was once held to be of use to authors. But that claim has on the whole been abandoned. It is now valued for its supposed use to readers. It is from that point

[1] *Function of Criticism.*
[2] *Pagan and Mediaeval Religious Sentiment.*
[3] *Last Words on Translating Homer.*

of view that I shall consider it here. For me it stands or falls by its power to multiply, safeguard, or prolong those moments when a good reader is reading well a good book and the value of literature thus exists *in actu*.

This drives me to a question which I never asked myself until a few years ago. Can I say with certainty that any evaluative criticism has ever actually helped me to understand and appreciate any great work of literature or any part of one?

When I inquire what helps I have had in this matter I seem to discover a somewhat unexpected result. The evaluative critics come at the bottom of the list.

At the top comes Dryasdust. Obviously I have owed, and must continue to owe, far more to editors, textual critics, commentators, and lexicographers than to anyone else. Find out what the author actually wrote and what the hard words meant and what the allusions were to, and you have done far more for me than a hundred new interpretations or assessments could ever do.

I must put second that despised class, the literary historians; I mean the really good ones like W. P. Ker or Oliver Elton. These have helped me, first of all, by telling me what works exist. But still more by putting them in their setting; thus showing me what demands they were meant to satisfy, what furniture they presupposed in the minds of their readers. They have headed me off from false approaches, taught me what to look for, enabled me in some degree to put myself into the frame of mind of those to whom they were addressed. This has happened because such historians on the whole have taken Arnold's advice by getting themselves out of the way. They are concerned far more with describing books than with judging them.

Thirdly, I must in honesty place various emotive critics who, up to a certain age, did me very good service by infecting me with their own enthusiasms and thus not only sending me but sending me with a good appetite to the authors they admired. I should not enjoy rereading most of these critics now, but they were useful for a while. They did little for my intellect, but much for my 'corage'. Yes, even Mackail.

But when I consider those (I exclude the living) who have ranked as the great critics I come to a standstill. Can I, honestly and strictly speaking, say with any confidence that my appreciation of any scene, chapter, stanza or line has been improved by my reading of Aristotle, Dryden, Johnson, Lessing, Coleridge, Arnold himself (as a practising critic), Pater, or Bradley? I am not sure that I can.

And how indeed could it be otherwise since we invariably judge a critic by the extent to which he illuminates reading we have already done? Brunetière's *aimer Montaigne, c'est aimer soi même* seems to me as penetrating a remark as I have ever read. But how could I know it was penetrating unless I saw that Brunetière had laid his finger on an element in my enjoyment of Montaigne which I recognise as soon as it is mentioned but had not sufficiently attended to? Therefore my enjoyment of Montaigne comes first. Reading Brunetière does not help me to enjoy Montaigne; it is my reading of Montaigne that alone enables me to enjoy Brunetière. I could have enjoyed Dryden's prose without knowing Johnson's description of it; I could not at all fully enjoy Johnson's description without having read Dryden's prose. The same holds, *mutatis mutandis*, for Ruskin's magnificent description of Johnson's own prose in *Praeterita*.[1] How should I know whether Aristotle's ideas about a good tragic plot were sound or silly unless I were able to say 'Yes, that is exactly how the *Oedipus Tyrannus* produces its effect'? The truth is not that we need the critics in order to enjoy the authors, but that we need the authors in order to enjoy the critics.

Criticism normally casts a retrospective light on what we have already read. It may sometimes correct an over-emphasis or a neglect in our previous reading and thus improve a future rereading. But it does not often do so for a mature and thoroughgoing reader in respect of a work he has long known. If he is stupid enough to have misread it all these years, it is probable that he will go on misreading it. In my experience a good commentator or a good literary historian is more likely, without a word of

---

[1] Cap. 12, para. 251.

praise or blame, to set us right. And so is an independent rereading in a happy hour. If we have to choose, it is always better to read Chaucer again than to read a new criticism of him.

I am far from suggesting that a retrospective light on literary experiences we have already had is without value. Being the sort of people we are, we want not only to have but also to analyse, understand, and express, our experiences. And being people at all—being human, that is social, animals—we want to 'compare notes', not only as regards literature, but as regards food, landscape, a game, or an admired common acquaintance. We love to hear exactly how others enjoy what we enjoy ourselves. It is natural and wholly proper that we should especially enjoy hearing how a first-class mind responds to a very great work. That is why we read the great critics with interest (not often with any great measure of agreement). They are very good reading; as a help to the reading of others their value is, I believe, overestimated.

This view of the matter will not, I am afraid, satisfy what may be called the Vigilant school of critics. To them criticism is a form of social and ethical hygiene. They see all clear thinking, all sense of reality, and all fineness of living, threatened on every side by propaganda, by advertisement, by film and television. The hosts of Midian 'prowl and prowl around'. But they prowl most dangerously in the printed word. And the printed word is most subtly dangerous, able 'if it were possible, to deceive the very elect', not in obvious trash beyond the pale but in authors who appear (unless you know better) to be 'literary' and well within the pale. Burroughs and the Westerns will snare only the mob; a subtler poison lurks in Milton, Shelley, Lamb, Dickens, Meredith, Kipling, or De La Mare. Against this the Vigilant school are our watchdogs or detectives. They have been accused of acrimony, of Arnold's 'obduracy and over-vehemence in liking and disliking—a remnant, I suppose, of our insular ferocity'.[1] But this is perhaps hardly fair. They are entirely honest, and wholly in earnest. They believe they are smelling out and checking a very great evil. They could sincerely say like St Paul, 'Woe to me if I preach not the gospel': Woe to me if I do not seek out vulgarity, superficiality, and false sentiment, and expose them wherever they lie hidden. A sincere inquisitor or a sincere witch-finder can hardly do his chosen work with mildness.

It is, obviously difficult to find any common literary ground on which we could decide whether the Vigilants help or hinder good reading. They labour to promote the sort of literary experience that they think good; but their conception of what is good in literature makes a seamless whole with their total conception of the good life. Their whole scheme of values, though never, I believe, set out

[1] *Last Words on Translating Homer.*

en règle, is engaged in every critical act. All criticism, no doubt, is influenced by the critic's views on matters other than literature. But usually there has been some free play, some willingness to suspend disbelief (or belief) or even repugnance while we read the good expression of what, in general, we think bad. One could praise Ovid for keeping his pornography so free from the mawkish and the suffocating, while disapproving pornography as such. One could admit that Housman's 'Whatever brute and blackguard made the world' hit off a recurrent point of view to a nicety, while seeing that in a cool hour, on any hypothesis about the actual universe, this point of view must be regarded as silly. One could, in a measure, enjoy—since it does 'get the feeling'—the scene from *Sons and Lovers* where the young pair copulating in the wood feel themselves to be 'grains' in a great 'heave' (of 'Life'), while clearly judging, as if with some other part of the mind, that this sort of Bergsonian biolatry and the practical conclusion drawn from it are very muddled and perhaps pernicious. But the Vigilants, finding in every turn of expression the symptom of attitudes which it is a matter of life and death to accept or resist, do not allow themselves this liberty. Nothing is for them a matter of taste. They admit no such realm of experience as the aesthetic. There is for them no specifically literary good. A work, or a single passage, cannot for them be good in any sense unless it is good simply, unless it reveals attitudes which are essential elements in the good life. You must therefore accept their (implied) conception of the good life if you are to accept their criticism. That is, you can admire them as critics only if you also revere them as sages. And before we revere them as sages we should need to see their whole system of values set out, not as an instrument of criticism but standing on its own feet and offering its credentials—commending itself to its proper judges, to moralists, moral theologians, psychologists, sociologists or philosophers. For we must not run round in a circle, accepting them as sages because they are good critics and believing them good critics because they are sages.

Meantime we must suspend judgement as to the good this school can do. But even in the meantime there are signs that it can do harm. We have learned from the political sphere that committees of public safety, witch-hunters, Ku Klux Klans, Orangemen, Macarthyites *et hoc genus omne* can become dangers as great as those they were formed to combat. The use of the guillotine becomes an addiction. Thus under Vigilant criticism a new head falls nearly every month. The list of approved authors grows absurdly small. No one is safe. If the Vigilant philosophy of life should happen to be wrong, Vigilance must already have prevented many happy unions of a good reader with a good book. Even if it is right we may doubt whether such caution, so fully armed a determination not to be taken in, not to yield to any possibly meretricious appeal—such 'dragon watch with unenchanted eye'—is consistent with the surrender needed for the reception of good work. You cannot be armed to the teeth and surrendered at the same moment.

To take a man up very sharp, to demand sternly that he shall explain himself, to dodge to and fro with your questions, to pounce on every apparent inconsistency, may be a good way of exposing a false witness or a malingerer. Unfortunately, it is also the way of making sure that if a shy or tongue-tied man has a true and difficult tale to tell you will never learn it. The armed and suspicious approach which may save you from being bamboozled by a bad author may also blind and deafen you to the shy and elusive merits—especially if they are unfashionable—of a good one.

I remain, then, sceptical, not about the legitimacy or delightfulness, but about the necessity or utility of evaluative criticism. And especially at the present. Everyone who sees the work of Honours students in English at a university has noticed with distress their increasing tendency to see books wholly through the spectacles of other books. On every play, poem, or novel, they produce the view of some eminent critic. An amazing knowledge of Chaucerian or Shakespearian criticism sometimes co-exists with a very inadequate knowledge of Chaucer or Shakespeare. Less and less do we meet the individual response. The all-important conjunction (Reader Meets Text) never seems to have been allowed to occur of itself and develop spontaneously. Here, plainly, are young people drenched, dizzied, and bedevilled by criticism to a point at which primary literary experience is no longer possible. This state of affairs seems to me a far greater threat to our culture than any of those from which the Vigilants would protect us.

Such a surfeit of criticism is so dangerous that it demands immediate treatment. Surfeit, we have been told, is the father of fast. I suggest that a ten or twenty years' abstinence both from the reading and from the writing of evaluative criticism might do us all a great deal of good.

EPILOGUE

IN the course of my inquiry I have rejected the views that literature is to be valued (*a*) for telling us truths about life, (*b*) as an aid to culture. I have also said that, while we read, we must treat the reception of the work we are reading as an end in itself. And I have dissented from the Vigilants' belief that nothing can be good as literature which is not good simply All this implies the conception of a specifically literary 'good' or 'value'. Some readers may complain that I have not made clear what this good is. Am I, they may ask, putting forward a hedonistic theory and identifying the literary good with pleasure? Or am I, like Croce, setting up 'the aesthetic' as a mode of experience irreducibly distinct both from the logical and the practical? Why do I not lay the cards on the table?

Now I myself don't think that in a work of this sort I am under any very clear obligation to do so. I am writing about literary practice and experience from within, for I claim to be a literary person myself and I address other literary people. Are you and I especially obliged or especially qualified to discuss what, precisely, the good of literature consists in? To explain the value of any activity, still more to place it in a hierarchy of values, is not generally the work of that activity itself. The mathematician need not, though he may, discuss the value of mathematics. Cooks and *bons viveurs* may very properly discuss cookery; it is not for them to consider whether, and why, it is important, and how important it is, that food should be deliciously cooked. That sort of question belongs to what Aristotle would call 'a more architectonic' inquiry; indeed to the Queen of the Knowledges, if there were now any undisputed pretendress to that throne. We must not 'take too much upon ourselves'. There may even be a disadvantage in bringing to our experience of good and bad reading a fully formed theory as to the nature and status of the literary good. We may be tempted to fake the experiences so as to make them support our theory. The more specifically literary our observations are, the less they are contaminated by a theory of value, the more useful they will be to the architectonic inquirer. What we say about the literary good will help most to verify or falsify his theories when it is said with no such intention.

Nevertheless, since silence might be given some sinister interpretation, I will lay on the table what few and plebeian cards I hold.

If we take literature in the widest sense, so as to include the literature both of knowledge and of power, the question 'What is the good of reading what anyone writes?' is very like the question 'What is the good of listening to what anyone says?' Unless you contain in yourself sources that can supply all the information, entertainment, advice, rebuke and merriment you want, the answer is obvious. And if it is worth while listening or reading at all, it is often worth doing so attentively. Indeed we must attend even to discover that something is not worth attention.

When we take literature in the narrower sense the question is more complicated. A work of literary art can be considered in two lights. It both *means* and *is*. It is both *Logos* (something said) and *Poiema* (something made). As Logos it tells a story, or expresses an emotion, or exhorts or pleads or describes or rebukes or excites laughter. As Poiema, by its aural beauties and also by the balance and contrast and the unified multiplicity of its successive parts, it is an *objet d'art*, a thing shaped so as to give great satisfaction. From this point of view, and perhaps from this only, the old parallel between painting and poetry is helpful.

These two characters in the work of literary art are separated by an abstraction, and the better the work is the more violent the abstraction is felt to be. Unfortunately it is unavoidable.

Our experience of the work as Poiema is unquestionably a keen pleasure. Those who have had it want to have it again. And they seek out new experiences of the same sort although they are not obliged to do so by their conscience, nor compelled by their necessities, nor allured by their interests. If anyone denies that an experience which fulfils these conditions is a pleasure, he may be asked to produce a definition of pleasure which would exclude it. The real objection to a merely hedonistic theory of literature, or of the arts in general, is that 'pleasure' is a very high, and therefore very empty, abstraction. It denotes too many things and connotes too little. If you tell me that something is a pleasure, I do not know whether it is more like revenge, or buttered toast, or success, or adoration, or relief from danger, or a good scratch. You will have to say that literature gives, not just pleasure, but the particular pleasure proper to it; and it is in defining this 'proper pleasure' that all your real work will have to be done. By the time you have finished, the fact that you used the word *pleasure* at the outset will not seem very important.

It is, therefore, however true, unhelpful to say that the shape of the Poiema gives us pleasure. We must remember that 'shape', when applied to that whose parts succeed one another in time (as the parts of music and literature do), is a metaphor. To enjoy the shape of a Poiema is something very different from enjoying the (literal) shape of a house or a vase. The parts of the Poiema are things we ourselves do; we entertain various imaginations, imagined feelings, and thoughts in an order, and at a tempo, prescribed by the poet. (One of the reasons why a very 'exciting' story can hardly elicit the best reading is that greedy curiosity tempts us to take some passages more quickly than the author intends.) This is less like looking at a vase than like 'doing exercises' under an expert's direction or taking part in a choric dance invented by a good choreographer. There are many ingredients in our pleasure. The exercise of our faculties is in itself a pleasure. Successful obedience to what seems worth obeying and is not quite easily obeyed is a pleasure. And if the Poiema, or the exercises, or the dance is devised by a master, the rests and movements, the quickenings and slowings, the easier and the more arduous passages, will come exactly as we need them; we shall be deliciously surprised by the satisfaction of wants we were not aware of till they were satisfied. We shall end up just tired enough and not too tired, and 'on the right note'. It would have been unbearable if it had ended a moment sooner—or later—or in any different way. Looking back on the whole performance, we shall feel that we have been led through a pattern or arrangement of activities which our nature cried out for.

The experience could not thus affect us—could not give *this* pleasure—unless it were good for us; not good as a means to some end beyond the Poiema, the dance, or the exercises, but good for us here and now. The relaxation, the slight (agreeable) weariness, the banishment of our fidgets, at the close of a great work all proclaim that it has done us good. That is the truth behind Aristotle's doctrine of *Katharsis* and Dr I. A. Richards's theory that the 'calm of mind' we feel after a great tragedy really means 'All's well with the nervous system here and now'. I cannot accept either. I cannot accept Aristotle's because the world has not yet agreed what it means. I cannot accept Dr Richards's because it comes so perilously near to being a sanction for the lowest and most debilitating form of egoistic castle-building. Tragedy, for him, enables us to combine, at the incipient or imaginal level, impulses which would clash in explicit action—the impulse to approach, and the impulse to shun, the terrible.[1] Quite. Just so when I read about the beneficence of Mr Pickwick I can combine (at the incipient level) my wish to give money and my wish to keep it; when I read *Maldon* I combine (at the same level) my wish to be very brave and my wish to be safe. The incipient level is thus a place where you can eat your cake and have it, where you can be heroic without danger and generous without expense. If I thought literature did this sort of thing to me I should never read again. But though I reject both Aristotle and Dr Richards, I think their theories are the right *sort* of theories, and stand together against all those who would find the value of literary works in 'views' or 'philosophies' of life, or even 'comments' on it. They place the goodness (where we actually feel it to be) in what has happened to us while we read; not in some remote and merely probable consequences.

It is only by being also a Poiema that a Logos

[1] *Principles of Literary Criticism* (1934), pp. 110, 111, 245.

becomes a work of literary art at all. Conversely, the imaginations, emotions, and thoughts out of which the Poiema builds its harmony are aroused in us by, and directed towards, the Logos and would have no existence without it. We visualise Lear in the storm, we share his rage, we regard his whole story with pity and terror. What we thus react to is something, in itself, non-literary and non-verbal. The literature of the affair lies in the words that present the storm, the rage, the whole story, so as to arouse these reactions, and in ordering the reactions into the pattern of the 'dance' or 'exercise'. Donne's *Apparition*, as Poiema, has a very simple but effective design—a movement of direct insult leads, unexpectedly, not into a climax of insult but into a reticence which is far more sinister. The material of this pattern is the spite which, while we read, we share with Donne. The pattern gives it finality and a sort of grace. Similarly, on a far larger scale, Dante orders and patterns our feelings about, and images of, the universe as he supposed, or partly feigned, it to be.

The mark of strictly literary reading, as opposed to scientific or otherwise informative reading, is that we need not believe or approve the Logos. Most of us do not believe that Dante's universe is at all like the real one. Most of us, in real life, would judge the emotion expressed in Donne's *Apparition* to be silly and degraded; even, what is worse, uninteresting. None of us can accept simultaneously

Housman's and Chesterton's views of life, or those of Fitzgerald's *Omar* and Kipling. What then is the good of—what is even the defence for—occupying our hearts with stories of what never happened and entering vicariously into feelings which we should try to avoid having in our own person? Or of fixing our inner eye earnestly on things that can never exist—on Dante's earthly paradise, Thetis rising from the sea to comfort Achilles, Chaucer's or Spenser's Lady Nature, or the Mariner's skeleton ship?

It is no use trying to evade the question by locating the whole goodness of a literary work in its character as Poiema, for it is out of our various interests in the Logos that the Poiema is made.

The nearest I have yet got to an answer is that we seek an enlargement of our being. We want to be more than ourselves. Each of us by nature sees the whole world from one point of view with a perspective and a selectiveness peculiar to himself. And even when we build disinterested fantasies, they are saturated with, and limited by, our own psychology. To acquiesce in this particularity on the sensuous level—in other words, not to discount perspective—would be lunacy. We should then believe that the railway line really grew narrower as it receded into the distance. But we want to escape the illusions of perspective on higher levels too. We want to see with other eyes, to imagine with other imaginations, to feel with other hearts, as well as with our own.

137

We are not content to be Leibnitzian monads. We demand windows. Literature as Logos is a series of windows, even of doors. One of the things we feel after reading a great work is 'I have got out'. Or from another point of view, 'I have got in'; pierced the shell of some other monad and discovered what it is like inside.

Good reading, therefore, though it is not essentially an affectional or moral or intellectual activity, has something in common with all three. In love we escape from our self into one other. In the moral sphere, every act of justice or charity involves putting ourselves in the other person's place and thus transcending our own competitive particularity. In coming to understand anything we are rejecting the facts as they are for us in favour of the facts as they are. The primary impulse of each is to maintain and aggrandise himself. The secondary impulse is to go out of the self, to correct its provincialism and heal its loneliness. In love, in virtue, in the pursuit of knowledge, and in the reception of the arts, we are doing this. Obviously this process can be described either as an enlargement or as a temporary annihilation of the self. But that is an old paradox; 'he that loseth his life shall save it'.

We therefore delight to enter into other men's beliefs (those, say, of Lucretius or Lawrence) even though we think them untrue. And into their passions, though we think them depraved, like those, sometimes, of Marlowe or Carlyle. And also

into their imaginations, though they lack all realism of content.

This must not be understood as if I were making the literature of power once more into a department within the literature of knowledge—a department which existed to gratify our rational curiosity about other people's psychology. It is not a question of knowing (in that sense) at all. It is *connaître* not *savoir*; it is *erleben*; we become these other selves. Not only nor chiefly in order to see what they are like but in order to see what they see, to occupy, for a while, their seat in the great theatre, to use their spectacles and be made free of whatever insights, joys, terrors, wonders or merriment those spectacles reveal. Hence it is irrelevant whether the mood expressed in a poem was truly and historically the poet's own or one that he also had imagined. What matters is his power to make us live it. I doubt whether Donne the man gave more than playful and dramatic harbourage to the mood expressed in *The Apparition*. I doubt still more whether the real Pope, save while he wrote it, or even then more than dramatically, felt what he expresses in the passage beginning 'Yes, I am proud'.[1] What does it matter?

This, so far as I can see, is the specific value or good of literature considered as Logos; it admits us to experiences other than our own. They are not, any more than our personal experiences, all equally

[1] *Epilogue to the Satires*, dia. ii, l. 208.

worth having. Some, as we say, 'interest' us more than others. The causes of this interest are naturally extremely various and differ from one man to another; it may be the typical (and we say 'How true!') or the abnormal (and we say 'How strange!'); it may be the beautiful, the terrible, the awe-inspiring, the exhilarating, the pathetic, the comic, or the merely piquant. Literature gives the *entrée* to them all. Those of us who have been true readers all our life seldom fully realise the enormous extension of our being which we owe to authors. We realise it best when we talk with an unliterary friend. He may be full of goodness and good sense but he inhabits a tiny world. In it, we should be suffocated. The man who is contented to be only himself, and therefore less a self, is in prison. My own eyes are not enough for me, I will see through those of others. Reality, even seen through the eyes of many, is not enough. I will see what others have invented. Even the eyes of all humanity are not enough. I regret that the brutes cannot write books. Very gladly would I learn what face things present to a mouse or a bee; more gladly still would I perceive the olfactory world charged with all the information and emotion it carries for a dog.

Literary experience heals the wound, without undermining the privilege, of individuality. There are mass emotions which heal the wound; but they destroy the privilege. In them our separate selves are pooled and we sink back into sub-individuality.

But in reading great literature I become a thousand men and yet remain myself. Like the night sky in the Greek poem, I see with a myriad eyes, but it is still I who see. Here, as in worship, in love, in moral action, and in knowing, I transcend myself; and am never more myself than when I do.

APPENDIX

A NOTE ON OEDIPUS

(see p. 62)

It is just possible that some will deny the story of Oedipus to be atypical on the ground that there have been societies in which marriages between parent and child were lawful.[1] The theory may find some support in those not uncommon myths which give the earth-goddess a young consort who is also her son. But all this is quite irrelevant to the story of Oedipus as we have it. For it is not a story simply about a man who married his mother, but about a man cruelly destined to marry his mother, unknowingly and unwillingly, in a society where such marriages were regarded as abominable. Societies, if there were any, which approved such marriages would be precisely the societies in which a story like that of Oedipus could never be told, because it would have no point. If marrying your mother is as normal as marrying the girl next door, it is no more sensational than marrying the girl next door and no more worth making into a story. We might perhaps say that the story is 'derived' from dim memories of an earlier age, or dim rumours of an alien culture, where there was no objection to marriage of parent and child. But the memory must have become so 'dim'—let us frankly say, so erroneous—that the old custom is not recognised as a custom at all and any remembered instance of it is mistaken for a monstrous

[1] See Apollodorus, *Bibliotheca*, ed. J. G. Frazer (Loeb, 1922), vol. II, pp. 373 *sq.*

accident. And the alien culture must be so alien that what is reported of it must be similarly misunderstood by the story-tellers. Otherwise the story, as we have it, is ruined—just as the story of Thyestes would be ruined if it were told about a society in which feeding a guest with the flesh of his own children were a recognised form of hospitality. The absence, even the inconceivability, of the custom is the *conditio sine qua non* of the story.